GANGS, OUTLAW BIKERS, ORGANIZED CRIME & EXTREMISTS

Who They Are, How They Work and the Threat They Pose

A FIELD MANUAL FOR LAW ENFORCEMENT

PHILIP J. SWIFT

43-08 162nd Street
Flushing, NY 11358
www.LooseleafLaw.com
800-647-5547

This publication is not intended to replace nor be a substitute for any official procedural material issued by your agency of employment nor other official source. Looseleaf Law Publications, Inc., the author and any associated advisors have made all possible efforts to ensure the accuracy and thoroughness of the information provided herein but accept no liability whatsoever for injury, legal action or other adverse results following the application or adoption of the information contained in this book.

Library of Congress — Cataloging in Publication Data

Swift, Philip J.

Gangs, outlaw bikers, organized crime & extremists : a field manual for law enforcement : who they are, how they work and the threat they pose / Philip J. Swift.

p. cm.

Includes index.

ISBN 978-1-60885-035-8

1. Gangs--United States--Handbooks, manuals, etc. 2. Organized crime--United States--Handbooks, manuals, etc. 3. Extremists--United States--Handbooks, manuals, etc. 4. Law enforcement--United States--Handbooks, manuals, etc. 5. Crime prevention--United States--Handbooks, manuals, etc. I. Title.

HV6439.U5S95 2012

364.1060973--dc23

2011046285

1st Printing 2011

2nd Printing 2013

Cover by *Sans Serif,* Saline, Michigan

Table of Contents

Dedication

To Bridget and Megan

Knowledge is the window through which we view the world. — Philip J. Swift

Acknowledgments

Special thanks are extended to the following people for making both their time and knowledge available to me. Without their assistance and guidance through the years, this field manual, and not to mention my professional success, would not have been possible.

Tim Carsola, Jaime Kafati, Randy Coleman, Michael Schaefer, Eric Rosenfeldt, Michael Billings, & Roberta Roena
Denver Sheriff Department

Mark Alhotz
Colorado Department of Corrections

C. J. Young
Freemont County Sheriff Office

Carl Adams & Tom Sullivan
Adams County Sheriff Office

Timothy Twining
Denver District Attorneys Office, Gang Unit

Robert Fuller
Denver District Attorneys Office

Tammy Tyler
2nd Judicial District, Adult Probation

Regina Huerter
City and County of Denver

Chris Schaefer
Colorado Bureau of Investigations

Jeffery Teti, Jim Dempsey, Jim Wattles (Ret.)
Denver Police Department

Mel Cobb
Aurora Police Department

Ramon Suares, *Correctional Corporation of America (Arizona)*

Johnny Santos, *G.R.A.S.P.* and Trudy Schaefer

Phil's professional law enforcement career started in 1997 as a CSO with the Adams County Sheriff Office. Since 1998, Phil has been employed as a deputy sheriff for the Denver Sheriff Department. Phil was a member of the DSD Emergency Response Unit from 1999 until 2005 and a member of the DSD Gang Intelligence Unit from 1999 until the present. As a member of the DSD Gang Intelligence Unit Phil designed and built the DSD Gang Database, developed the position of "Gang Investigator" and was the first deputy assigned to the DSD Gang Intelligence Unit full time. In 2005 Phil was promoted to the rank of sergeant.

Sgt. Swift has an AAS and B.S. in Criminal Justice and a dual Masters in Management and Human Resources. Phil is currently pursuing a Masters in Forensic Psychology with the goal of obtaining a Ph.D. Phil's book, "Cradle to Grave," (a gang management book) was published in 2005. Phil is an adjunct Criminal Justice Instructor and instructs statewide as well as nationally in the areas of Gang and Security Threat Group Enforcement. In the past, he has taught courses related to Human Resources and Internal Affairs. Phil currently instructs at the Denver Sheriff Department Training Academy in the areas of Gangs and Security Threat Groups, Contraband.

In the Fall of 2009, he filmed an episode of "Gangland," which aired on March 5, 2010 and was titled "Mile High Killers." Phil was the featured gang expert in this episode.

Phil is currently assigned to the Gang Intelligence Unit.

Dear Reader:

I became a Denver Deputy Sheriff on August 18, 1998, and was promoted to the rank of Sergeant in February 2005. Shortly after graduating from the Academy I found myself working the main floor of the Denver County Jail. During my first few days as a Deputy Sheriff I realized the county jail was designed to house a little less than 1,500 inmates but was regularly stuffed with more than 2,000. To say the least, I was overwhelmed not only by the job ahead of me, but by the sheer number of inmates that required supervision on a daily basis.

I also discovered in those first couple of days on the job that on average almost 40 percent of the inmates that are sentenced to the Colorado Department of Corrections pass through the doors of the Denver County Jail. With this fact in mind, I found myself faced with some of the most disruptive and violent inmates requiring supervision and management. Although most of the inmates are easy to manage, it seems like the worst of what Colorado has to offer passes through the Denver County Jail on a regular basis, which requires the application of unique and unconventional management techniques.

Shortly after my appointment to the Denver Sheriff Department I decided to apply to the Gang Unit in the hope that an appointment would offer me greater opportunities and new challenges as well as a better understanding of the inmates themselves and how they operate and function while incarcerated. To my surprise I was appointed to the Gang Unit in late 1999 with little more than a year's experience as a Denver Deputy Sheriff.

I soon discovered that my introduction to gang culture and structure was going to be up to me for a variety of reasons, including, but not limited to, budget constraints, a lack of training opportunities, and the fledgling nature of the Gang Unit. I found myself moving through my first year with the Gang Unit not only wide-eyed and bewildered, but a little misguided. My many blunders, stumbles, and outright failures are now quite amusing; but at the time it was frustrating and at times outright dangerous. I don't know how I got through those first years without getting myself killed or seriously injured.

My lack of training and experience during my first couple of years as a Gang Unit deputy was one of the most aggravating obstacles to overcome; however, it was not my bane. The biggest problem that I faced during this period, and still face today, was the lack of a common, easy-to-use, and accurate reference source of established gang information.

In those first couple of years, and even today, I find that nothing was or is as time consuming as digging through piles of paperwork or hundreds of websites looking for credible information. Something as simple as which sides of the body (left or right) Folk Nation gang members affiliate with and dress can be hard to find when there is not a reference source that can be easily accessed. It is this problem that motivated me to design and create this field manual. It is my hope that you will find this field manual an accurate and user-friendly source of general gang information and specific advanced information.

Sincerely,
Philip J. Swift

Gang and Security Threat Group History in Modern America

At a basic level, all gangs and security threat groups (STGs) are formed for one or more of the following reasons:

1. Protection of its members;
2. Protection of the members' neighborhood or area (otherwise known as turf);
3. Execution of criminal activity;
4. Religious, political, or cultural reasons.

Even though all gangs and STGs are started for basically the same reasons, each gang or group's individual history is unique in its own way. How gangs and STGs are created, run and developed can be better understood by studying the history of some of the larger gangs and STGs on a macro level. The following pages of this chapter will describe the basic ways gangs and STGs form and how they grow and change. It will also explore the different types of gangs and STGs as well as groups that are gangs by definition, but not generally thought of as either gangs or STGs.

Types of Gangs and STGs

- **Gang (traditional)**: Two or more individuals that may or may not be organized who commit delinquent or criminal activities that share a common name, theme, or look.

- **Gang (revised)**: Two or more individuals that may or may not be organized that commit delinquent or criminal activity and may or may not have a common name, theme, or look, but are involved in furthering of the groups criminal activity.

- **Security Threat Group (traditional)**: An individual or a group of people that have a common disruptive goal, who may share a common belief and are confined to a correctional facility.

- **Security Threat Group (revised)**: An individual or a group of people that have a common disruptive goal, may share a common belief, may or may not also be dedicated to furthering criminal activity and are confined to a correctional facility. (Security threat group is abbreviated STG,)

Although STGs and gangs are similar in definition, there are two major differences in the groups. The first difference is their location. Gangs are located in the community, while STGs are located in correctional facilities. The second difference is that an STG can be made up of only one person whereas a gang must have two or more members.

Furthermore gangs and STGs can be broken into two subtypes:

1. **Traditional**: A traditional gang or STG is generally made up of related members. Each member's family typically will have been involved in the gang or STG for more than one generation. This involvement may only have been a loose association; however, this involvement is important to membership of future generations. Very rarely will a traditional gang or STG take on members that are not related to or well-known by present or previous members. Traditional gangs and STGs will be made up of fathers, sons, cousins, grandfathers, mothers, daughters, brothers, and sisters. True traditional gangs or STGs will be both multigenerational as well as cross-generational. Examples of traditional gangs and STGs are the Mexican Mafia, Asian Pride Gang, and La Nuestra Familia.

2. **Nontraditional**: Nontraditional gangs and STGs make up the majority of the known gangs and groups. Members of nontraditional gangs and STGs are not usually multigenerational or cross-generational. Although members may be related, this occurrence is far less common. Nontraditional gangs and groups often create new subsets of original gang or group. These types or subsets of gangs and groups often grow at an alarming rate because of their wide recruiting practices and willingness to expand. Examples of nontraditional gangs and STGs are the Crips, the Bloods, and the Aryan Brotherhood.

General Gang and Security Threat Group Hierarchy

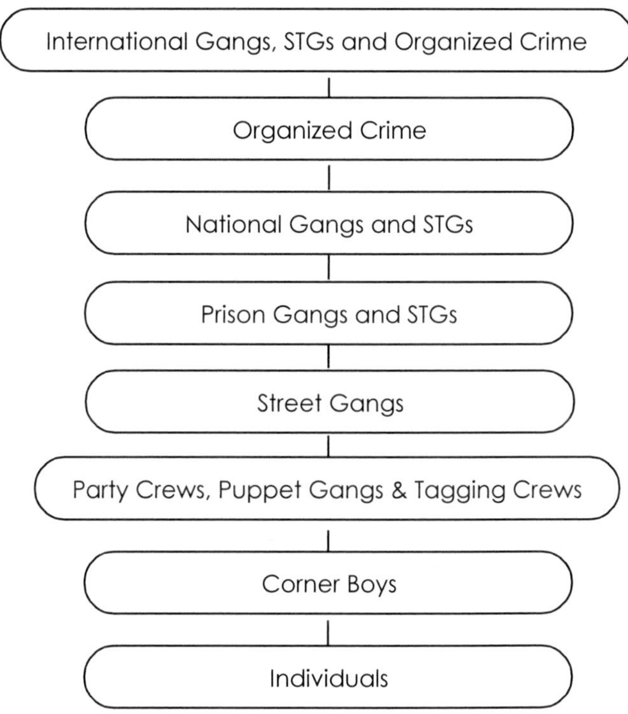

Individuals – All gangs and security threat groups start with individuals. All gangs and security threat groups started with a small number of friends and acquaintances who for whatever reason decided to take part in criminal activity. The individual criminal is by no means as dangerous as a loosely organized criminal body; however, several individuals taking part in limited "group" criminal activity can prove to be very destructive.

Corner Boys – Corner boys are small groups of individuals that hang out and associate with each other within plain view of those in their communities. Corner boys are involved in street level crimes that are more opportunistic than premeditated and are generally poorly executed by the group's members. At this level, these types of gangs are semi-organized yet only loosely dedicated to each other or to the group as a whole. It is also at this level that many "turf" style gangs find their roots.

Puppet Gangs – Puppet gangs are generally well organized, often mimicking the larger gangs and STGs that they affiliate with. The key to classifying this type of gang or group is the fact that they have a "parent" gang or group they exclusively affiliate with. Puppet gangs are involved with all levels of criminal activity while committing crimes and carrying out activities that benefit and further the goals of their parent gang and group. Puppet gangs act as an insulator between the parent gang and law enforcement, and serve as a fertile recruiting ground for the parent gang.

Tagging Crews – Tagging crews are the wild card of the gang and STG hierarchy. Tagging crews can be unorganized, semi-organized, organized, or well organized. They can also appear to be similar to puppet gangs and street gangs in the way they act and function. The identifying factor that sets tagging crews apart from other gangs and groups is the goal of the tagging crew is to apply their groups identifying marking throughout their cities by using the medium of graffiti.

Party Crews – Party crews are similar to tagging crews because they often act as a recruiting ground for street gangs. However, unlike tagging crews, party crews are semi-organized, or organized. Party crews are mainly involved in the production of illegal underground parties (similar to raves) promoting not only a club environment, but in some cases prostitution, underage drinking, and both drug use and sales. Of course, it is from these parties that these groups acquire most of their income. Although there is competition between different party crews there have been only a few reported incidents of any serious violence between rival groups.

Street Gangs – Street gangs are unique from other groups in two different ways. First, they are unique because of how the term "Street Gang" is applied by the public, the media, and law enforcement. Second, they are unique because of how they have developed over time. Since the term street gang invokes different images, it is important to understand what a street gang truly is. The common definition of a street gang is, "Two or more individuals that may or may not be organized that commit delinquent or criminal activity and may or may not have a common name, theme or look, but are involved in furthering criminal activity."

This definition encompasses two types of groups that are generally referred to as street gangs: traditional street gangs and non-traditional street gangs. The terms traditional street gangs and non-traditional street gangs are defined in the following ways:

a. *Traditional (Street) Gangs:* Traditional gangs are multi-generational gangs that are made up of members from the same basic cultural and/or ethnic makeup. In these gangs we may find that a member's brothers, father, grandfather, and great-grandfather are all members of the same gang or umbrella gang. Traditional gangs are also deeply rooted within their communities and tend to expand slowly through the natural migration of people in those communities rather than through an organized plan or strategy. Example of traditional gangs would be Sureño 13 cliques. Many Sureño 13 cliques are made up of members that are part of two or three different generations extending from pre-teens to great-grandfathers and grandmothers.

b. *Nontraditional (Street) Gangs:* Nontraditional gangs are street gangs where the members do not generally share cultural or ethnical similarities. Members of these gangs tend to be only second generation, if there are any family ties at all, and for the most part members of these groups are not related to reach other directly. Nontraditional gangs often migrate as a means of accruing new turf because they are not generally rooted in a specific community. It is this migration that allows nontraditional street gangs to spread quickly through communities, states, and the country.

Prison Gangs and Security Threat Groups – Prison gangs and STGs can be semi-organized, organized, or well organized. In general, most prison gangs and security threat groups are at a minimum organized with the majority of these groups being well organized. The leadership of these gangs and groups tends to be highly sophisticated and self-sufficient and in many cases designed along the lines of both paramilitary groups and Fortune 500 companies. Prison gang or security threat groups can be considered the board of directors that overlooks and controls, through their directions, how each franchise (street gang) operates.

It is also fair to say that these groups are generally divided along racial lines with a group representing each of the major races within the inmate culture. There are normally four different races represented by prison gangs and security threat groups: African American (the Black Guerrilla Family, the Family, and the Brothers of the Struggle); Hispanic (the Mexican Mafia, the Gallant Knights Insane, the Barrio Azteca); Hispanic Nationals (La Nustra Familia and the Border Brothers); and, Caucasian (the Aryan Brotherhood, the 211 Crew, and the Nazi Low Riders). Asian prison gangs are starting to develop across the country, however, they have yet to reach the same levels as the others have and are not represented by a unifying prison gang at this time.

National Gangs and Security Threat Groups – National gangs and STGs are organized and well-organized criminal organizations and are generally made up of members of a single racial or ethnic background with branches throughout the country. To be fair, the only difference between a national gang or security threat group and an organized crime family like the Gambino family is that national gangs and security threat groups still portray themselves as street thugs and maintain a power base within the prison systems and ghettos in which they originated.

Organized Crime – Organized crime is a term used to label a variety of different criminal bodies throughout the country and the world. This term has been applied to groups from outlaw motorcycle gangs to software piracy rings. Although these groups are organized and well organized, it is not their ability to so function that gives them this label; rather, it is the inner weaving of legitimate and illegitimate enterprises that draws the term "organized crime." Another key component of an organized crime group is that their membership carries out its own criminal activity, separate from the organization with permission and directions from the leadership, and then returns a portion of the funds created by their individual criminal activity to the organization.

What truly sets a classic organized crime group apart from a gang or a security threat group is that organized crime groups have a well-defined membership, and they tend to function through the means of associates rather than directly through their membership. Although there are exceptions, members of organized crime groups do not share a common look in the same manner of gang and security threat groups. Rather, organized crime groups share themes or a set of standards that are generally upheld by the communities in which these groups operate.

International Gangs, Security Threat Groups, and Organized Crime – International gangs, security threat groups, and national gangs have branches, businesses, or interests throughout the world. Examples of these types of groups are the Italian and Russian mafias with less evident examples including the "Big Six" outlaw motorcycle gangs and South American drug cartels. These international groups tend to be very well organized and are heavily invested in both legitimate and illegitimate businesses.

Umbrella Gang Concept

Bloods

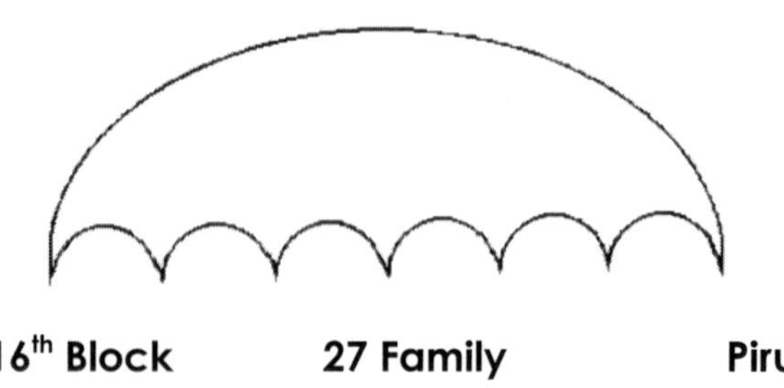

16th Block 27 Family Piru

104th Street Crenshaw Mafia Gangsters

Mexican Mafia

Sureño 13

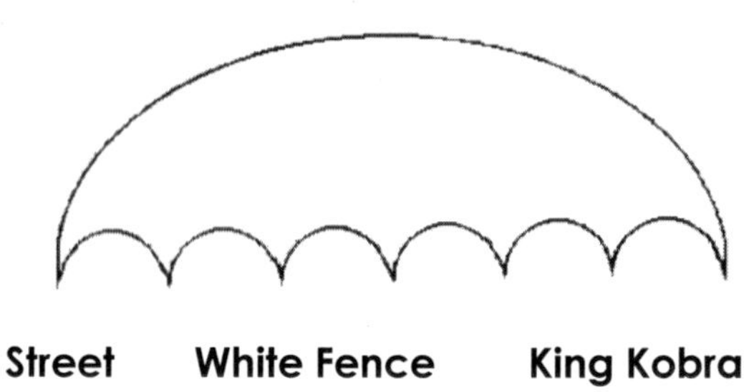

18th Street White Fence King Kobras

Young Mexican Gangsters

Common examples of Umbrella Gangs include, but are not limited to, the Crips, Bloods, La Nuestra Familia, Mexican Mafia, People/Folk Nations, Sureño 13, and Norteño 14.

Note: Although gangs like the Crips and the Bloods are examples of Umbrella Gangs, they do not answer to or pay taxes to the Umbrella Gang in the same manner Sureño 13 gangs based out of California and some other states do to the Mexican Mafia. Although minor, this distinction is critical in understanding how these gangs operate.

Religious Cults Hierarchy

Religious cults have a similar hierarchy to those of gangs and security threat groups in the sense that there are several layers with directions being handed down from the top; however, they are different enough to mandate a separate explanation. The only real difference between a gang/STG and religious cults is that cults have a shared religious belief and are not involved in the same type of criminal activity as gangs and STGs. This does not mean that cults do not carry out criminal activity simply that they do not do it in the same manner as a gang or STG. Cults often fit into the same definition as gangs and STGs, but as a society we do not view them in the same manner.

The following is an example of the typical pyramid style hierarchies employed by religious type cults to maintain control of both dedicated (hardcore) members and associated (associate/hang around) members. The leader is a single person who is viewed as a "supreme authority." These leaders often claim to receive guidance, authority, and/or power directly from a higher religious power. It is not uncommon for these leaders to represent themselves as an "appointed leader," a "resurrected religious icon," or a "prophet."

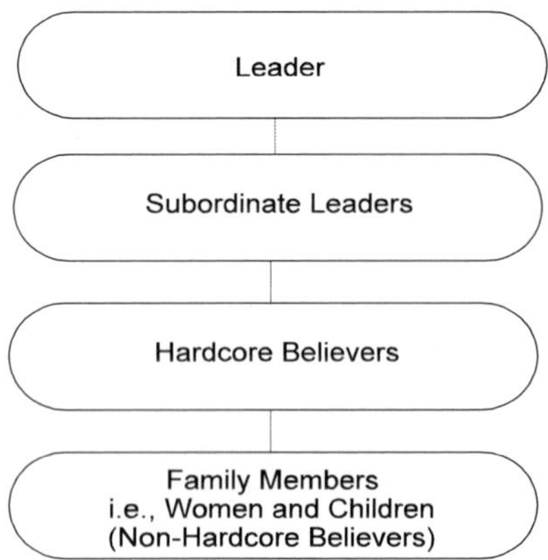

Growth Patterns of Gangs and STGs

The following eleven growth patterns are the most common growth patterns among gangs and STGs. Gangs and STGs will follow these growth patterns at different stages of their development and may change from one to another quickly without forewarning.

The Political Movement – The change from gang or security threat group to that of a political movement may seem far-fetched. However, there are numerous examples of this occurring with some of the most powerful gangs and security threat groups throughout the country. When gangs and security threat groups first started entering politics they tried to influence voters through grassroots movements or through the bribery of certain officials. When this failed to get "their man" elected or "their man" failed to support the gangs criminal activity once elected, gangs and security threat groups started running their own candidates for political office. Because these new candidates were in fact gang or security threat members, their loyalty could be guaranteed even after election.

The following examples are of gangs and security threat groups that have tried and in some cases been successful at entering politics. This list offers limited examples of the political activity of gangs and security threat groups. The gang or group intentions for entering politics are not evaluated in this text; rather, the gangs or groups actual entry into politics is described as an example only of this type of activity. It is the right of all American citizens to become involved in the political process. In no way am I inferring that any eligible person should be banned from the political process based on his or her beliefs or involvement with any group or organization.

a. Before his death, William Pierce, the leader of the National Alliance and author of the "Turner Diaries," was heavily involved in Washington D.C.-based politics. It is rumored that he used these connections to maximize business dealings that furthered his racist views and hate speech.

b. Jeff Fort, the leader of the P-Stone Rangers (Nation) and later of the El Rukns, received just over a million dollars in federal "anti-poverty" funds from 1960 – 1970 for his grassroots political movement. These funds were believed to have been funneled into the P-Stone Ranger (Nation) criminal activity. As a side note, Jeff Fort was also invited to the White House by Richard Nixon due to his local political involvement.

c. Larry Hoover, the leader of the Gangster Disciples, created a non-profit political movement called "Growth and Development." This group has sponsored many candidates for local offices throughout the country.

d. Outlaw motorcycle club members have been seen throughout the country at different political rallies supporting local and national candidates. This act is as much to show support for the candidate is it is to create a positive public image for the motorcycle club itself.

e. The Avenue Boys and the Avenue Cribs (predecessor of the Crips) were involved in the Black Panther Party in the California area in the 1960s.

f. The Conservative Vice Lords were heavily involved in local politics and community development in the 1960s – 1970s, until their leader was arrested for murder and sent to prison.

g. There is a well-documented and colorful history of the country's different mafia groups supporting candidates through both legal and illegal means for decades.

h. White supremacist, anti-government groups, and militias have gone as far as creating "common law courts," used to produce illegal leans, arrest warrants, foreclosures, miscellaneous documents, and death sentences to harass non-members. These groups often also run their own candidates for office.

Legitimization – The legitimization of a criminal organization is the result of massive money laundering that takes place to cover up the illegal profits of criminal activity. Once a gang or a security threat group reaches a certain income level they are forced to invest their illegal income in legitimate businesses. The money is then returned to the gang or security threat group in the form of profit or as payments for fictitious or overly inflated services. One of the biggest problems with money laundering is that it requires a high cash flow business that sells few products or a very creative banker/broker to disguise the activity.

This process can take decades, with some of this country's oldest criminal organizations still finding themselves somewhere in the middle of the process. Outside of the country's original crime families, outlaw biker gangs are the next fastest group evolving in this manner and will continue to evolve as these groups grow internationally. Parts of the Folk Nation, mainly the Gangster Disciples and the People Nation, mainly the Latin Kings, are starting to feel the pressure of legitimization and will continue to for years to come.

The Mafia Structure – As a gang or security threat group grows it reaches a certain point where strict control is needed to carry out criminal activity. When strict controls are set up within a gang or security threat group they are commonly said to be an organized crime entity. When gangs and security threat groups rise to the level of becoming an organized crime body they will start to take on the characteristics of the classic Italian Mafia. These characteristics include, but are not limited to:

a. A "Don," president or gang boss.
b. A governing body.
c. A ranking structure for members.
d. A strict set of rule and guidelines.
e. A procedure for carrying out discipline.
f. A common goal that the entire gang or security threat group works towards.
g. The execution of individual criminal activity by members with only the permission of the leadership.

One of other key changes that is seen when a gang or security threat group takes on a mafia structure will be the willingness to carry out criminal activity with anyone who could benefit the group. Old road blocks such as racism, street rivalries, and other "petty differences" are set aside in the name of business. These types of groups will use violence less often then they used to. However, when they do become violent the violence is guided, swift, and brutal.

Examples of gangs and security threat groups that have adopted the mafia structure are limitless. Some of the more well-known gangs and security threat groups with this type of structure are the Mexican Mafia, the Latin Kings, the Gangster Disciples, the Aryan Brotherhood and the Barrio Aztecas, to name a few.

The Headless Snake – What is a "headless snake"? There is a gang enforcement tactic called "cutting the head off the snake," which means arresting the gang's or group's leadership. A headless snake, by definition, is a gang or security threat group that is capable of functioning without a structured or definitive leadership. Examples of gangs and security threat groups that are considered headless snakes are:

a. The Crips
b. The Bloods

Rebirth – The idea of the rebirth of a gang or security threat group occurs in three main scenarios. The first scenario is when a gang or security threat group decides to restructure itself because of a variety of reasons. The second scenario involves a decision of the members to rename a dying or extinct gang or security threat group to pursue criminal activity under a new name or structure. The third scenario of rebirth occurs in one of two ways. Either the rebirth occurs when street gang members enter the correctional system and the gang becomes a security threat group that is managed by incarcerated members with members inside and outside of the correctional system. Alternatively, a rebirth can also occur when the number of incarcerated street gang members entering a correctional system reaches the point that the gang is considered a security threat group. Examples of gangs that have been reborn are as follows:

a. The Crips
b. The Bloods
c. The Gangster Disciples
d. The Latin Kings
e. The El Rukns
f. The Gallant Knights Insane

Expansion – Expansion is a rather simple concept. It simply refers to the growth of a gang or a security threat group. Expansion, like other types of changes that take place in gangs and security threat groups, happens in several ways. The first way that gang or security threat group expansion takes place is when a gang or group migrates into a new area. The second form of expansion takes place when a prison gang or security threat group begins carrying out criminal activity on the street with a purpose other than supporting the criminal activity in the correctional facility. The third type of expansion takes place when a gang or security threat group outgrows its original turf or area of operation. The fourth type of expansion takes place when a gang or security threat group merges with another gang or security threat group. In the criminal culture, Outlaw Motorcycle Gangs are good examples of this type of activity. It is not uncommon for a larger Outlaw Motorcycle Gang to recruit a smaller club to either become a puppet club or to change over, "patching over," and become the larger club's local chapter.

Local Emergences – Local emergence refers to the creation of new gangs or security threat groups either in communities or in the correctional system. Local emergences are possible and probable anywhere in the country or the world no matter how high the crime rate or how prevalent the gang activity.

Organized Crime – As long as there have been gangs and security threat groups, organized crime groups have been using them to carry out criminal activity. Street gangs are willing to carry out criminal activity for organized crime groups in the hopes that their actions will be seen as a favor to be repaid later.

Prison gangs and security threat groups will often refuse to act against organized crime figures during their incarceration or will offer protection to those same people, with the hope that the favor will be returned. In the larger picture, as gangs or security threat groups grow and become involved in higher levels of criminal activity they are forced to interact with organized crime groups as a matter of survival.

Terrorist Arm – It is a documented fact that gangs and security threat groups are tied to terrorist organizations in ever-growing ways. It is important to keep in mind that although there are some instances of cooperation between gangs, security threat groups, and terrorist organizations based on a common ideology, in most cases cooperation is based on a mutually beneficial financial arrangement. The following examples provide some insight into the types of cooperation that has been uncovered by different law enforcement agencies:

a. Members of European-based White supremacist groups have attended terrorist training in Middle Eastern terrorist training camps, in other words "my enemy's enemy is my friend."
b. Members of al Qaeda cells are believed to be training at guerrilla camps in South America and working with members of Hispanic street gangs to gain access to the United States. Once the cell members have entered the United States, it is believed these same Hispanic street gangs help to funnel both money and supplies to the cell.
c. Although not a terrorist group, the Black Panther Party is believed to have used Black street gang members to carry out criminal activity in the 1960s and 1970s.

d. At the beginning of the "War on Terrorism" and the invasion of Afghanistan, the Taliban increased its production of poppy seed plants and then opium along with other Middle Eastern countries in order to support its war effort. This increase of opium made almost every gang and security threat group in the world a supporter of terrorism through their narcotics sales.
e. Jeff Fort, the leader of the El Rukns, was arrested for attempting to carry out "terrorism for hire" activity for Libya inside of the United States.

Gang and Security Threat Group Co-dependence Model

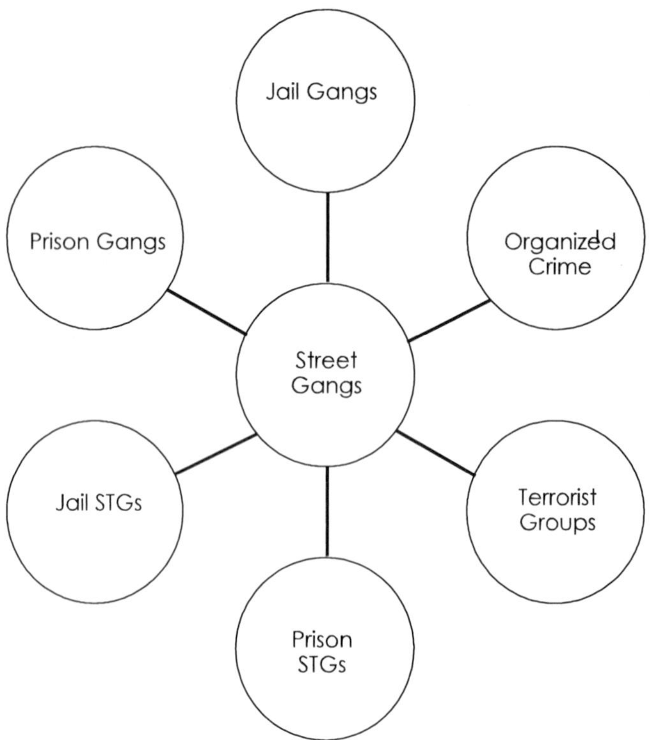

Each of these groups depends on street gangs in some way to carry out and support ongoing criminal activity within the United States and the world.

Gang and STG Member Types and Type Hierarchy

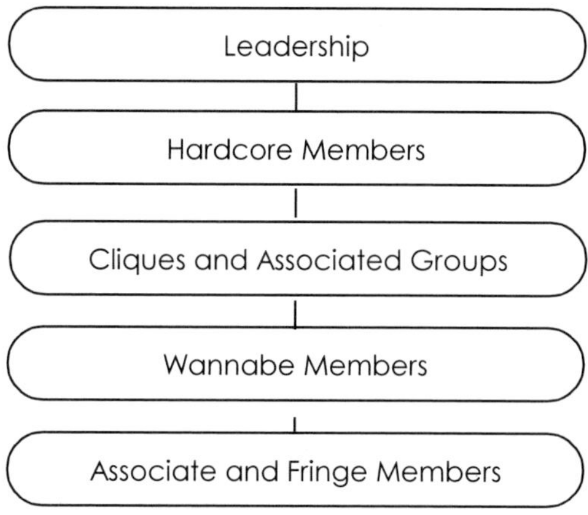

Leadership members – The main duty of the leadership members is to oversee the gang's or group's legal and illegal activities. Leadership members are only concerned with the overall health of the gang's or group's activities, rather than being involved with the day-to-day decision making. Some leaders are part of a leadership group similar to a board of directors, while other gangs or groups are led by a single leader as a dictatorship. No matter what style of leadership is used by a gang or group, the leader(s) is/are normally the most vicious, underhanded, cunning, and intelligent member(s) of the gang or group.

Hardcore members – Hardcore members are the type of gang or STG members that most people think of when the term "gang members" is used. It is these members who fulfill the stereotypes of the street gang member. These members are generally heavily tattooed, extremely dedicated, and loyal to the group, with a true allegiance to the group's style, culture, and success. Hardcore members will be involved with the management of the group's daily activity and will have a large amount of operational knowledge about the group.

Clique members – Clique members of a gang or security threat group are as dedicated to the gang or group as hardcore members, but have not proven themselves completely to the gang's or group's leadership. Thus, they join subsets or cliques that are supporters of a "parent gang." The ultimate goal of clique members is to become a recognized member of a parent gang or security threat group.

Wannabe members – Wannabe members are individuals who lack the attributes desired for group membership. However, they "hang out" with members of a gang or security threat group because they want to become recognized members of a gang or security threat group.

Associate members – Associate members are individuals who do not claim membership in a gang or group, but are deeply involved with a gang's or security threat group's criminal activity. Associate members are trusted by the gang or group leadership and are used to extend the gang's or group's reach both within gang culture and in the criminal world.

Associated and Fringe members – Associated and fringe members are individuals who are not heavily involved with gang or security threat group activity, but are accepted by a gang or group as general associates and support the overall goals or philosophy of the group. Fringe members rarely wear gang or group colors and usually will not have any gang or group specific tattoos.

Gang and Security Threat Groups General Racial Makeup

Gang or Security Threat Group	General Racial Makeup
Aryan Brotherhood	Caucasian
Asian Boy Crips	Asian
Asian Pride	Asian
Barrio Azteca	Hispanic
Black Gangster	African American
Black Gorilla Family	African American
Bloods	African American
Border Brothers	Hispanic
Crips	African American
Folk Nation	Mixed mainly Hispanic and African American
Gallant Knights Insane	Hispanic
Gangster Disciples	African American
Hermanded De Pistoleros Latinos	Hispanic

Gang or Security Threat Group	General Racial Makeup
People Nation	Mixed mainly Hispanic and African American
Outlaw Motorcycle Gangs	Mixed mainly Caucasian and Hispanic
Mexican Mafia	Hispanic
MS 13	Hispanic
Nazi Low Riders	Mixed (no African Americans)
North Side Mafia	Hispanic
Norteño 14	Hispanic
La Nuestra Familia	Hispanic
Latin Kings	Porte Rican and Hispanic
Skinhead	Mixed
Skinheads – Raciest	Caucasian
Sureño 13	Hispanic
Tagging Crews	Mixed
Tango Blast	Hispanic
Texas Syndicate	Hispanic
Tiny Rascals	Cambodian
Vice Lords	African American
White Supremacist	Caucasian

Identifying Gangs and Security Threat Groups Members

With all of the above information about the different types of gangs and STGs the basic question remains, which is, how do you identify a gang or STG member? The answer is that gang and STG members can be discovered through three categories of markers or signs. Once you have identified these markers or signs, they can be assessed in order to determine the likelihood of a person being a gang or security threat group member. These markers and signs are generally used in the creation of contact cards, which law enforcement use to determine gang or group membership. A list of these markers or signs and examples from each category follow:

1. **Style of dress**
   a. *Color of clothing*
   b. *Type of clothing*
   c. *Style of clothing*
   d. *Brand name of clothing*
   e. *The way in which clothing is worn*

2. **Tattoos**
   a. *Type of tattoo*
   b. *Style of tattoo*
   c. *Symbolism of tattoo*
   d. *Color of tattoo*
   e. *Placement of tattoo*

3. **Mannerisms**
   a. *Body language*
   b. *Body posture*
   c. *Type of speech/speech pattern/word usage*
   d. *Dance/dance styles*

Common Gang and Security Threat Group Clothing

Common generalized clothing:

1. Sport jerseys with numbers, letters and colors that correspond to a gang's or STG's name i.e., football jerseys, basketball jerseys and NASCAR.

2. Large amounts of clothing in a color that corresponds to a gang's or STG's color i.e. blue, red, purple, gold and black.

3. Ball caps with numbers, letters and colors that corresponds to a gang's or STG's name i.e. Georgia Tech, UNLV and Rockies.

4. Hats worn turned to the left or the right.

5. Shoes laced in a manner so that the laces form roman numerals that correspond to the gang's or STG's name i.e. XIII (13 – reading from the toe of the shoe to the top of the tongue).

6. Brand of clothing that corresponds to a gang's or STG's name or maybe unique to that gang's or groups "uniform" i.e., British Knights, Dickies, Doc Martin Boots and FUBU.

7. Clothing accessories that correspond to a gang's or STG's name or color i.e. bandanas, bracelets, belt buckles, and color of laces.

Gang Specific Clothing Examples:

Crips: Rockies clothing, Dodger clothing, anything blue or with a "C" on it, British Knights shoes, bandanas hanging from the left pocket.

Bloods: Anything red or with a B or P on it, 49ers clothing, bandanas hanging out of the right pocket.

Folk Nation: Varies based on gang or set. Dress to the right i.e. turn hats to the right.

Gallant Knights Insane: Rockies and Georgetown and anything with the color purple on it.

Norteño 14 and North Side Mafia: 49er, Nebraska Corn Huskers, Nautica and UNLV clothing, anything red or with the number 14 on it.

Outlaw Motorcycle Gangs: "three patch" club colors, 1% patch, motorcycle type clothing, "support" clothing and accessories i.e. "Support you local club."

People Nation: varies based on gang or set. Dress to the left i.e. turn hats to the left.

Skinhead: Doc Martin Boots, braces, fatigue pants, white T-shirts and flight jackets.

Sureño 13: Dodgers, Raiders, South Pole clothing, anything blue, and anything with a 13 or an 18 on it.

Gang Specific Colors (by color):

Black	Green	Purple
MS 13	*Crips*	*Gallant Knight*
18th Street	*Spanish Cobras*	*Insane*
	White Supremacist	*Grape Street Crips*
	Latin Kings	

Blue
18th Street
Crips (general)
Sureño 13 (general)
Tiny Rascals
Oriental Street Boys
MS 13
White Supremacist
Latin Kings

Grey
Tiny Rascals

Orange
EMS (Tagging Crew)

Green, Black & Yellow
Asian Boys

Red
Bloods (general)
Fresno Bull Dogs
North Side Mafia
Norteño 14 (general)
Northern Structure Gangs (general)
Spanish Vice Lords

Silver
18th Street

Gold & Red
Bandidos

Black & White
Oldies 13
Outlaws
Mongols

White
White Supremacist

Black & Blue
Gangster Disciples Family

Black & Red
North Side Mafia
Vice Lords

Red, Black & White
Main colors of People Nation Gangs

Black & Gold
Latin Kings

Red & Blue
Los Solidos

Blue, Green & Black
Main colors of Folk Nation Gangs

Blue & White
Mara Salvatrucha (MS-13)

Red & White
Hells Angels
Sons of Silence

Note: This list is not all-inclusive and is subject to change. This list is designed to give the reader examples of gang colors. A review of local gangs is necessary to determine what colors are affiliated with which gang or group in any specific area.

Common Gang Related Tattoo, Symbols, Graffiti and Marks

My Crazy Life

Tear Drop

5150

Mentally Unstable / Insane

Trust No One

MOB

Money Over Bitches

FTW

Fuck the World

FTP

Fuck the Police

N/S

North Side

E/S

East Side

S/S

South Side

W/S

West Side

Common Gang Mannerisms

Body Language and Posture:

The Folk and People Nation are two examples of gangs that have gang specific body language and posture. This type of behavior is not limited to the Folk and People Nation therefore it is important to become familiar with the gangs and STGs in your area to determine if they have a specific body language and or posture.

Folk Nation – Gang members that belong to or are affiliated with the Folk Nation will stand with their left arm crossed over their right (protecting the left hand and keeping it closest to the heart) and with their right foot slightly in front of the left (making the right foot superior to the left foot.)

People Nation – Gang members that belong to or are affiliated with People Nation will stand with their right arm crossed over their left (protecting the left hand and keeping it closest to the heart) and with their left foot slightly in front their right (making left foot superior to the right foot.)

Type of Speech, Speech Patterns and Word Usage:

The most common example of this category is the use of slang and abbreviations used by gangs and STGs. The following is a select list of abbreviations that are commonly used by gang and STG members.

187	Murder
211	Armed Robbery
213	Sureno (Southern California)
5150	Mentally Ill or Crazy
AB	Aryan Brotherhood
ALKQN	Almighty Latin King and Queen Nation

AN	Aryan Nation
ANP	American Nazi Party
BA	Barrio Azteca
BB	Border Brothers
BGD	Black Gangster Disciples
BGF	Black Guerrilla Family
BIP	Blood in Peace
BK	Blood Killer (Crip)
BLK	Block
CCR	Compton Crip Riders
CK	Crip Killer (Blood)
CMG	Crenshaw Mafia Gangster
ELF	Earth Liberation Front
eMe	Mexican Mafia
eNe	La Nuestra Familia
E/S	East Side
GD	Gangster Disciples Growth and Development
GKI	Gallant Knights Insane
HA	Hells Angels
KKK	Ku Klux Klan
LK	Latin Kings
MOB	Money Over Bitches Member of Bloods
NF	La Nuestra Familia

NLR	Nazi Low Riders
NOR	Norteño 14
N/S	North Side
OK	Oldies Killer
O13	Oldies 13
SK	Slob Killer Sureño Killer
SNM	Sindicato Nuevo Mexico The New Mexico Syndicate

The following lists contain several common examples of slang words that are used by gangs and STGs to disrespect their enemies as well as to respect their own gang or STG. This type of disrespect is common among almost every gang and STG in the country.

Bloods	Bobo (Coco), Crab (Crip), Blood (Brother)
Crips	Blocc (block), Blacc (black), Slob (Blood), Cuz (Brother)
Folk Nation	Hook (People Nation)
Gallant Knights Insane	Stinka (Inca Boy)
Inca Boys	Goofy (GKI), Monkey (NSM)
Norteño 14	Surat (Sureño 13), Scrap (Sureño 13)
North Side Mafia	Nik Nack (Kicking Back) and Sewer rat (Sureño)
People Nation	Glazed Donut (Gangster Disciple)

White Supremacist	Mud people (people other than whites) Race Trader (someone who married outside of their race)

Common Dance/Dance Styles:

The following are examples of dances or dance styles that were originally credited to or associated with a specific gang or group.

Crip Walking, Clown Walking or C-Walking	Crips
Mosh Pits or Slam dancing	White Supremacists
Throwing hands signs while dancing	All street gangs

2 – African-American Street Gangs and Security Threat Groups

Introduction

When the discussion of African-American gangs arises, the gangs that most commonly come to mind are the Crips and the Bloods. The reason for this has to do both with their proliferation throughout the United States and the world as well as the massive amount of media coverage these two groups have been given both in the mainstream and on the silver screen.

With this stated, it must also be stated that the Crips and the Bloods are not the end all of the African-American gangs and STGs by any sense. Gangs and STGs such as the Black Guerilla Family, New Black Guerilla Family, 415s, D.C. Boys, varieties of Folk and People Nation sets, not to mention the extremely violent Jamaican gangs round out the multitude of African-American gangs and STGs that make up the African-American gang culture. Each and every one of these aforementioned groups represents a true and present danger to the community in which they operate. However, due to the above-mentioned proliferation of the Crips and the Bloods the majority of this chapter contains information revolving around these two gangs.

Note: Folk and People Nation gangs and STGs are covered separately in following chapters.

Crip Affiliated Gangs

1st Street West Coast Crips
4th Street Crips
5 Leaf Bud
5 Leaf Gangsters
7th Street Watts
8 Ball Crips
9th Street Hustlers
10th Ave. PJ Crips
10 Top Hustler Crips
12th Avenue Crips
12th Street Crips
21st St Gangsters
23rd Street
25th Street Crips
31st East Side Mob
32 Posse Crips
42nd Street
43rd Street
44 Acers
52 Hoover
55th Avenue Crips
74 Hoover Crips
77 Green
81st East Side Kitchen
81st Hustlers
83 Hoover
87 Gangster Crips
98 Main Street Crips
102 East Side Crips
102nd Street East
107 Hoover
113 Block
118 East Coast Crips
187 Anybody Killers
209 Lao Crips
300 Block Monroe St.
332 Crips
357 Crips
510 Oakland Crips
916 Lao Crips
A-Mountain Crips
AC 357 Crips
Acacia Block
ACOLM Crips
Almighty Crip Gangsters
Anybody Killa Gangsters
Anybody Murders
Aurora Lynch Mob
Avalon
Baby Regulators
Bannana Blocc
Bilby Street Crips
Bite the Dust
Black Ghetto Tribe
Black Hole Posse
Black Mafia
Black Tragedy
Blue Crown Crips
Bridge Side Crips
Broadway Gangsters
C Down
Carver
Carver Park
Carver Park Compton
Chicago Geer
Chique 30's
Compton Crips
Compton Crip Riders
Compton Villa
Cop Killing Crips
Crazy Ace Posse
Crazy Oriental Crips
Crip East Side Clique
Crip Kings
Crip Nation
Cripettes (Female)
CVC
Death Storm Troopers
Denver Heights Crips
Deuce Seven Family Crips
Dog City
Dodge City Crips

Donna Street
Durroc Crips
East Coast Gangster Crips
East Side 47th Street
East Side Crips
East Side Gangsters
East Side Kitchen
East Side Mafia
East Side Outlaw Crips
Eight Ball
Eight Trey Gangsters
Five Deuce
Flocc
Four Corner Block
Fudge Town Crips
Front Hood
Fuller Park
Gambino Family Crips
Gangster Crips
Garden Block
Geer Gang
Geer Garden
Ghost Town
Gilriver Insane Crips
GLT
Grape Street
GQ Crips
Hamo Tribe
Harbor City
Hard Time Gangsters
Hard Time Hustlers
Harlem 30's
Harlem Crips
Harlem Godfathers
Harlem Mafia
Hip Hop
Hoe Hop
Hoover Gangsters
Hoover Criminals
Hoover Crips
Horton Boys
Imperial Village
Indian Creek Posse Crips
Insane Crips
Insane Gangster
Insane Family
Lalu Pride Crips
Lay Low Crips
Linda Vista
Lindo Park Crips
Local Latino Crips
Loked Out Crips
Long Beach
Lynch Mob
Madman Crips
Making Cash Money
Main Street
Manzanita Crips
Maryvale Crips
Midtown Crips
Mile High Crips
Montghetto 60's
Money Hustl'n Crips
Money Making Gangster Crips
Money Murder Gangster Crips
Most Gangster Crips
Most Hated Gangster Crips
Most Valuable Pimps
Most Valuable Players
Neighborhood Crips
North Side Crips
No Face Killer Crips
Nutty Block
Nutty Block Compton
Old School Crips
Oriental Mob Crips
Original Block Crip Gang
Original Gangster Crips
Original Laotian Gang
Osage Legend
OST Crips
Palmer Blocc Crips
Park Village
Paybacc Crips
Pimp Style Hustlers
Playboy Gangster

Players Inc
Pomona
Poor Boy Gangsters
Posse Crips
PTH
Quarter Moon Gangsters
Queen Loc Crips
Raider Mafia Crips
Raymond Avenue
Rodric Crips
Roll'n 20's
Roll'n 30's
Roll'n 40's
Roll'n 60's
Roll'n 80's
Roll'n 90's
Roll'n 100's
Roll'n Deuce Gangsters
Rough Tough Somali Crips
Royal Crown Crips
Royal Latin Crips
Ruthless Ass Gangsters
Sable Blocc Crip
Salt Lake Posse
Salem
Santana Block
School Yard
Shadow Crips
Shotgun
Solo Gangster Crips
Sons of Samoa
South Side Crips
Stick Mafia
Sun Valley Crips
Swampton
Syndicate Family
Tiny East Side Crips
Tiny Oriental Crips
Tonga Gangster Crips
Tongan Crip Gang
Tongan Style Gang
Tragniew Park
Trey Deuce Posse
Trey Eight Crips
Trey Five Outlaws
Trey Four Gangster
Trey Seven
Trey Trey 33rd Street
Trey Trey Gangster
Trips Crips
Truest Crips
Water front
Watergate Gangsters
Watts Baby Loc Crips
West Coast 20s
West Coast 30s
West Side City Crips
West Side Crips
West Side Raymond Avenue
West Side Roll'n 60's
West Side 211 Crips
White Street Mob
World Class
Young Blue Babie

Note: The majority of the Crip sets listed above are made up mainly of African-American members, but, in some cases, sets may have members from other ethnic backgrounds. Also included are gangs, such as the Chique 30's (Denver), that are mainly made up of Hispanic members. Gangs such as these are included in this section because they are Crip sets.

Blood Affiliated Gangs

004 Hoodsman Clique
5 Deuce Pueblo Bishop
16th Block Bloods
21st
25st
26th Piru
27th Street Piru
45 Brim Bloods
57th Street
59 Brim Bloods
68 Neighborhood Piru
77 Bloods
79 Swan Bloods
93 Gangster Bloods
104 Avenue Piru Gangs
104 Inglewood Family Mafia
104th Street Crenshaw Mafia Gangsters
109th St. Denver Lanes
111 Mafia
135 Piru
145 Neighborhood Piru
151 Piru
183
303 East Side Bloods
456 Island
706 Bloods
7991 Bloods
781 Family
805 Piru
1017 Brick Squad
1090 Block Boyz Mohawk
Athens Park Boys
Aurora Pirus
Avenues
Bell Side Bloods
Big Boy
Bishops
Black Disciples Bloods
Black P-Stones (CA)
Blood Stone Piru 30s
Blood Stone Piru 40s
Blood Stone Villains
Bloodettes
Bounty Hunter Bloods
Butler Block Piru
Butler Park Piru
Cambage Patch Bloods
Campanella Park
Center Park
Center View Piru
Chicano Gangster Bloods
Chi-Town Bloods
Circle City
Circle City Piru
Compton Piru
CNP Blood
Crenshaw Mafia Gangsters
Dalton Gangsters Bloods
Denver Lanes
Deuce Nine Family Bloods
Deuce Seven Bloods
Deuce Six Bloods
Devil's Angels Bloods
Dog Posse
Doty Block Gangsters
Double I Bloods
East Compton Piru
East Side Bloods
East Side Pain
East Side Piru
East Side Piru 44th Street
Elm Street Piru
East Side Posse
Eastside Longtown Bloods
Edith Street Posse
Emerald Hills Bloods
Family Swan Bloods

Five Nine Brims
Fruit Town Brims
Fruit Town Piru
Gangster Killer Bloods
Hacienda Village Bloods
Harvard Park Piru
Hathorne Piru
Highland Court Crew
Hilltop Bloods
Hit Squad Brims
Holly Blood Gang
Holly Hood Piru
Homicide Gangster Bloods
Inglewood Family Bloods
Irvington Bloods
Killer Gangster Bloods
Klick Klack
Krasy Chicano Bloods
L.A. Brims
L Gang Bloods
Latino Gangster Bloods
Leuders Park Hustlers
Leuders Park Piru
Lime Hood
Lincoln Park
Lincoln Park Pirus
Long Beach Crip Killer
Lot Boys
Mafiosa Bloods
Mad Dog Bloods
Mad Stone Bloods
Meadow Brook
Messy Minners Bloods
Miller Gangster Bloods
Mob Piru
Mohawk Boyz
Murderville
Neighborhood Roll'n 20's
Nine Trey Gangsters Bloods
Nines
North Side Bloods
Ocean Valley Bloods
One Eight Trey
Original Block Piru
Original Front Hoods
Outlaw 20's
P Block
Pacoima Bloods
Park Hill Bloods
Park Nine Bloods
Pasadena Denver Bloods
Pasadena Lanes
Piru
Project Gangsters
Pueblo Bishop Bloods
Pueblos
Queen Street
Red Bloods
Redman Bloods
Renegade Outlaw Loco Bloods
Roll'n 20s
Roll'n 30 Outlaws
Roll'n 50s Bloods
Roll'n 50s Brims
Set Tripper Sex Money Murder Bloods
Sick Minded Bloods
Six Deuce
Samoan Bloods
Satan's Bloods
Savage Gangsters
Scotts Dale Piru
Skyline
South Dale Bloods
South Park Bloods
South Side Posse
South Side Familia
South West Bloods
Swan
Tiny Oriental Bloods
Tip Top Piru
TLG

Tramp Killers
Tree Top Piru
United Blood Nation
Valentine Bloods
Van Ness Gangsters
Village Town Piru
Vista Bloods
Water Front Piru
Watts Bloods
West 7th Avenue
West Side CMG
West Side Blood
West Side Piru
West Side Roll'n 30
Western Hill Bloods
Western Hills Pose Bloods
Outlaw Bloods
Young Bloods
Young Oriental Gangsters Bloods

Note: The majority of the Blood sets listed above are made up mainly of African-American members, but, in some cases, sets may have members from other ethnic backgrounds. Also included are gangs such as the West Side Bloods (Denver) that are mainly made up of Hispanic members. Gangs such as these are included in this section because they are Blood sets.

Crip Tattoo, Symbols, Graffiti, and Marks

Blood Killer

Colorado Rockies
(Used by Crips)

Trey Trey Crips
(Colorado)

Trey Trey Crips
(Colorado)

Grape St.
(National)

BLOCC

Block

CCRider

Compton Crip Rider
(National)

Roll'n

Roll'n 30's 60's 100's
(National)

ETG

Eight Trey Gangster (National)

34

Trey Four (Colorado)

32

Trey Deuce (Colorado)

Blood Tattoo, Symbols, Graffiti, and Marks

CK

Crip Killer

BIP

Blood in Peace

Blood

Blood

CMG

Crenshaw Mafia Gangster

10-4

Tens and Fours (104th St, CMG)

104th

104th Street (104th St. CMG)

II

Double I Bloods (East Coast)

104%

104 Percent (104th St. CMG)

Redman

Redman Blood (National)

Piru

(National)

27

Deuce Seven Bloods (Colorado)

Bounty Hunter

(National)

Roll'n	**DAMU**	**MOB**
(Roll'n Bloods)	Swahili for Blood	Member of Bloods (National)

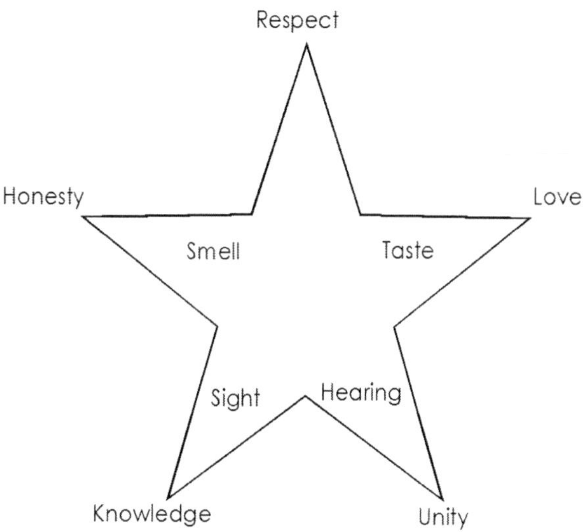

(Five-Pointed Star of the United Blood Nation)

General Crip and Blood Street Gang History

THE HISTORY OF THE CRIPS

Type of Gang:	Non-Traditional
Founded:	Approximately 1969
Founded by:	Raymond Washington and Stanley "Tookie" Williams in L.A., California.
Original name:	Avenue Cribs: Baby Cribs
Originally affiliated with:	The Black Panther Party
General ethnic makeup:	African American
Main rivals:	Bloods

Key historical events:

Originally operated in an around Freemont High School.

Name was changed to Crips in approximately 1970–1971.

Raymond Washington was killed in 1979 (possibly by a fellow Crip).

Introduction of "crack" caused the migration of the Crips throughout the United States.

Members took part in the 1993 Gang Summit in Kansas City leading to the creation of the Crip Nation.

Original East Side and West Side Crip Divisions in Los Angels California

When Stanley "Tookie" Williams and Raymond Washington first formed the Crips, Tookie's gang was considered a "West Side" gang and Raymond's gang was considered an "East Side" gang. After the formation of the Crips, Crip sets located on the west side Los Angeles California's Harbor City Freeway (I-110) claimed the West Side, and Crip sets located on the east side of the Harbor City Freeway (I-110) claimed the East Side. This is no longer true, and Crip sets claiming the East and West Side can be found throughout most cities with little geographic significance attached to an East or West Side designation of the set.

The History of the Crip Name

Research indicates the Avenue Cribs became the Crips in one of the following eleven ways.

Story One

The original members of the Avenue Cribs attended John C. Freemont High School in Los Angeles, California. The school instituted a strict dress code for students attending football games to control problems within the student body. Members of the Avenue Cribs started wearing top hats and carrying canes to the games, to not only meet this dress code, but to poke fun at the dress code. It is believed that people started calling them Cripples or Crips because of the canes. For whatever reason, the name stuck and was adopted by the Avenue Cribs as their new official title.

Story Two

The term Cribs and Crips sound so much alike that people outside of the gang mistakenly started referring to the Avenue Cribs as Crips. The name then stuck and was adopted by the gang.

Story Three

Raymond Washington is reported to have started using the term "Crips" or "Crip" in graffiti in 1970 when referring to his gang. Although the reason for his actions are unknown, a simple answer may be that he was showing disrespect to a new rival of the Crips called the Bloods by inverting the Bs in the word Cribs.

When you turn a lower case B upside down it looks like a lower case P forming the word "Crips" instead of "Cribs."

Story Four

One of the original members of the Avenue Cribs was disabled after a car accident. Out of respect for this original member, the gang's name was changed to Crips in reference to the disabled or "crippled" member.

Story Five

The name may also have changed when new members were asked to cripple a rival gang member as a show of loyalty and initiation into the gang.

Story Six

Crips may also be a simple misspelling of the word Crypt. One story reports that members of the gang took the word Crypt from what was then a popular horror comic book called "Tales from the Crypt" in the hope that their new name would instill fear in those that heard it.

Story Seven

It is my belief that this story is by far the most unlikely; however, it is one that seems to get passed around a lot. Original members of the Avenue Cribs wanted to be thought of as the toughest gang around. In doing so, someone pointed out that the comic book hero Superman was the toughest person ever. Everyone knew the only thing that can hurt Superman is Kryptonite, and, therefore, the gang wanted to be named after the one thing that could hurt the toughest known man in the world. The term Kryptonite was then shorted to Krypt or Crip.

Story Eight

Story eight ties the Avenue Boys and the Avenue Cribs to the Black Panther movement in California in the 1960s and 1970s. There is some evidence that the Avenue Boys were involved in carrying out criminal activity for the Black Panther Party. Some of this work was then passed down to the Avenue Cribs in order to insulate both the Avenue Boys and the Black Panther Party from law enforcement. The story goes the Avenue Boys and the Avenue Cribs quickly became involved in the political ideals and beliefs of the Black Panther Party. These ideals caused the

Avenue Boys and the Avenue Cribs to change their name to the Crips, which was an acronym for Community Reconstruction (or Rehabilitation or Revolution) In Progress and to change their goals from maintaining a criminal enterprise to rebuilding their communities. This story goes on that the Crips grew so large and had so much power that other gangs, mainly the Bloods, drew them into a turf war and back into a gang mentality rather than a political movement. As nice as this story sounds, it fails to address the Crips involvement in the crack trade or their willingness to fight other Crip sets for both turf and control of the narcotics trade.

Story Nine

As this story goes, an *L.A. Times* writer wrote a story about the Avenue Cribs and their history. However, the reporter accidentally misspelled the word Cribs and referred to the gang as the Avenue Crips. Due to the wide circulation and mainstream readership of the *L.A. Times*, the majority of people started using the name Avenue Crips when referring to the Avenue Cribs. The name became so common place the gang simply changed their name to the Crips rather than trying to correct the typo.

Story Ten

This story simply states that people mistook the word Cribs for Crips when they heard people referring to Avenue Cribs because of street lingo and slang. Once again, the term Crips became so widely used that the gang decide to change their name. The main difference between this story and Story Two is that the explanation hinges on the ignorance or lack of command of the English language by the gang members themselves. This story may simply be an offshoot of the belief that gang members are not educated or smart. In the end it is up to the reader to decide if you want to buy into the stereotype of gang members.

Story Eleven

This story states that Raymond Washington's older brother suffered from leg problems and was forced to use crutches. It goes on to say that Raymond's brother was called a crip (short for cripple) and began to write CRIP on his "Chuck Taylor" shoes. Out of respect for Raymond's brother the gang became known as the Crips. This story may simply be another version of Story Four.

The History of the Bloods

Type of Gang:	Non-Traditional
Founded:	Approximately 1970
Founded by:	An alliance between the Pirus, L.A. Brims, Denver Lanes, and other gangs
General ethnic makeup:	African American in L.A. California.
Main rivals:	Crips

Key historical events:

Originally operated in and around Centennial High School, L.A., California.

Compton Pirus founded in approximately 1970.

Compton Pirus went to war with the Compton Crips in 1972.

Crips stomp an L.A Brim member to death outside of a basketball game in the early 1970s.

Introduction of "crack" caused the migration of the Bloods throughout the United States.

Members took part in the 1993 Gang Summit in Kansas City creating the Blood Nation.

The United Blood Nation is founded in Rikers Island, New York in the early 1990s.

The History of the Blood Name

It is not clear why or how this gang alliance became known as the Bloods or why they used the color red. Just like the Crips, there are several stories about how and why they decided to use the color red and call themselves Bloods. As previously stated, it is up you to decide how much credit you give any of these stories.

Story One

It is believed that at the time the Bloods were formed the Crips were already using the color blue and wearing blue bandanas as a symbol of their gang association. The newly formed Bloods needed a way to distinguish their members' alliance. In the 1970s, the two most common colors of bandanas on the streets and in the California Department of Corrections were red and blue. As mentioned, the Crips were already using the color blue so the Bloods chose to carry and display red bandanas.

Story Two

New alliance members had to injure or "bloody" a rival gang member to show loyalty to the gang, thus creating the name Bloods.

Story Three

Alliance gangs decided as a group to call themselves Bloods. The color of blood is red so they decided to use and display red bandanas.

Story Four

Alliance gangs decided as a group to use the color red. Blood is the color red so they decided to call themselves Bloods.

Story Five

One of Centennial High School colors is red. The Compton Pirus were founded by Sylvester "Pudding" Scott, a Centennial High School student. The Pirus also had the largest membership in the gang alliance, and, therefore, decided to use the color red. Soon after the alliance was formed, Blood gangs inside of Compton were simply called Pirus. Blood sets formed outside of Compton used the name Blood much like a franchise name to show alliance to the Pirus. Examples of this are the Bounty Hunter Bloods and 104th Street Crenshaw Mafia Gangsters Bloods, both of which were started outside of Compton, California.

Story Six

The term "Blood" was a commonly used slang turn used by African Americans during the 1960s and early 1970s. Due to the common use of this term and the use of the color red by this alliance of gangs, the alliance became known as the Bloods.

Story Seven

During a 2010 "Peace Rally" in Denver, Colorado, a speaker by the name of Sup Nova Slom stated the word BLOOD stands for: "Brotherly Love Overpowering Oppressive Destruction."

The History of the East and West Coast Rivalry (Crips and Bloods)

"Why are East Coast and West Coast factions of the Bloods and the Crips street gangs' bitter rivals when both organizations would benefit as a whole by creating a national and international criminal organization?"

Many mainstream experts point to the rap rivalry between East Coast and West Coast record labels. This rivalry is believed to have led to the deaths of rap stars Tupac and Biggie Smalls. This rivalry may have led to the death of these two rappers; however, it does not explain the hatred between East Coast and West Coast Crip and Blood gangs, or their failure to organize.

After many interviews and research, this hatred seems to stem in part from the alliance of some Blood and Crip gangs with the People and Folk Nations. Some gang members point to the 1993 Kansas City Gang Summit as the starting point of these new alliances. I, however, feel that this hatred was generated long before 1993, and there is sufficient evidence to support this conclusion.

No matter why or how some Blood and Crip gangs started to align with the People and Folk Nation, old timers or Original Gangsters (O.G.s) Crips and Bloods do not condone their gangs showing respect to men like Larry Hoover, the leader of the BGDs and the Folk Nation. O.G. California members of both the Crips and the Bloods see the alliance with the Folk and People Nation as disrespectful to the founding members of their gangs. The statement "Hail King Hoover" spoken by a Crip gang member is seen as disrespectful to founding members such as Raymond Washington and Stanley "Tookie" Williams. It is this disrespect, along with many other reasons, that has led to the hatred between East Coast and West Coast factions of the Crips and the Bloods.

Colorado-based Crip Street Gangs History (flow

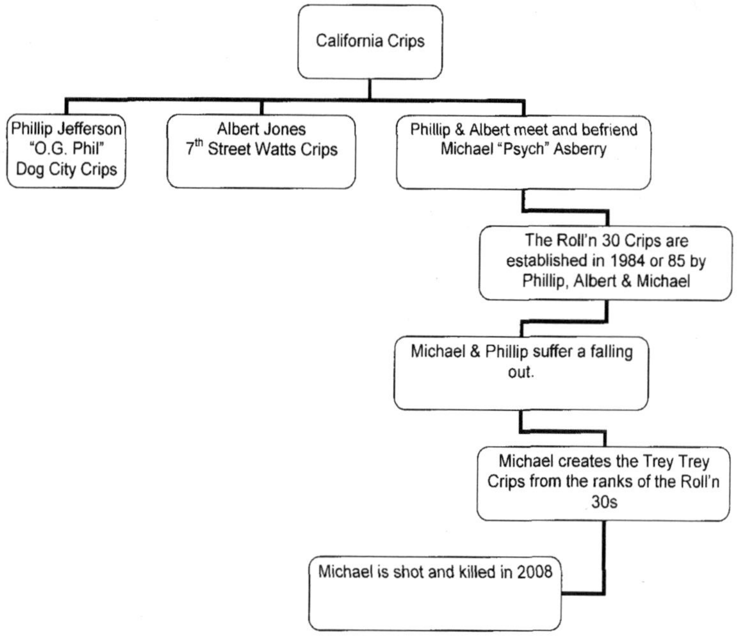

Other African-American Gang and Group History

The Black Guerilla Family "BGF"

Type of Gang: Non-traditional

Founded: 1966

Founded by: George L. Jackson in San Quentin State Prison

General racial makeup: African American

Main rivals: Aryan Brotherhood, the Mexican Mafia, and other Hispanic gangs.

Major historical events:

BGF is a revolutionary minded Maoist/Leninist/Marxist group. Originally known as the Black Family of the Black Vanguard.

Affiliated with the Black Liberation Army, the Symbionese Liberation Army, and the New Afrikaans Movement.

1971—George L. Jackson is killed during a prison uprising.

Late 1980s and early 1990s—formed an alliance with the Crips, Bloods, 415s, and the BGD.

Late 1980s and early 1990s—became infused with former members of the Crips, Bloods, 415s, and the BGDs.

Late 1980s and early 1990s—two factions are formed. The Northern BGF made up of members of the Bloods and 415s; and the Southern BGF made up of members of the Crips and the BGDs.

Early 1990s—became affiliated with the New Afrikaans Revolutionary Nation (NARI).

African-American Gang and STG Hierarchies

United Blood Nation Hierarchy

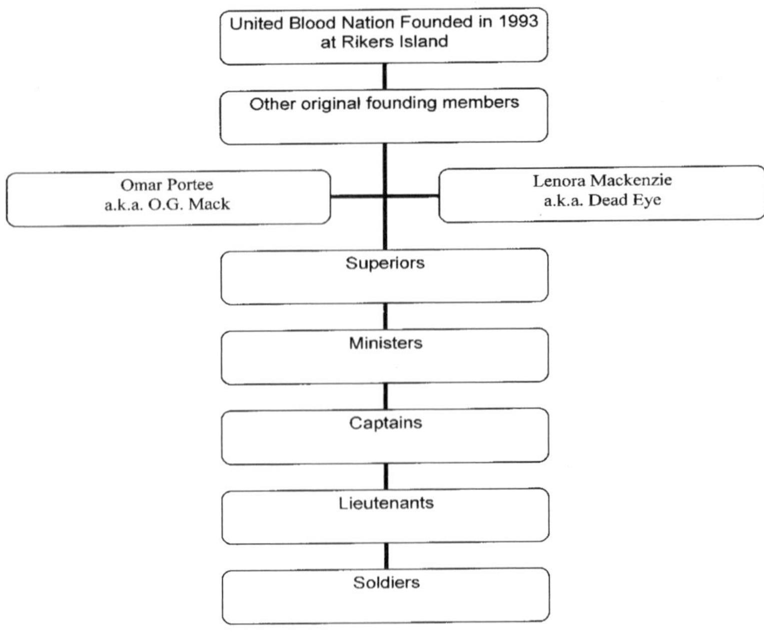

Note: The United Blood Nation was founded and is primarily located on the East Coast.

The Original Black Guerrilla Family Hierarchy

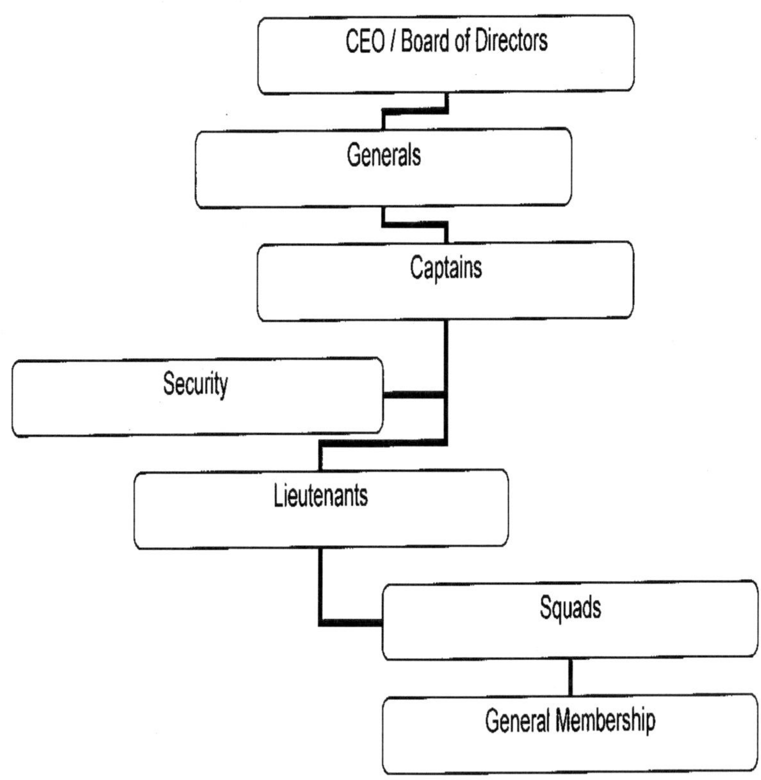

The Original Black Guerrilla Family Hierarchy

Ansar El Muhammad Gang
Black Guerrilla Family
Black Rider Liberation Party
El Ruk
New Black Guerrilla Family

Introduction

There are three major facts about Asian gangs that make them different than other gangs. The first fact is that, generally speaking, Asian street gangs historically divide themselves along racial lines. There are street gangs throughout the United States representing every major Asian ethnic group that include, but are not limited to, Cambodians, Vietnamese, Hmongs, Chinese, and Laotians. There are exceptions to this rule, of course, and they include gangs such as the Asian Boy Crips and Asian Pride, which accept members from diverse ethnic backgrounds as long as the person is of Asian descent.

The second fact is that the majority of Asian gangs that were started from the 1970s through the 1990s have close ties to Asian organized crime syndicates. This connection is generally via criminal Tongs and Triads. This does not necessarily mean they work directly for these syndicates or take orders directly from them; rather, they have a mutual understanding about the type of criminal activity the gang will take part in and where that activity will be carried out.

The third and final major fact that makes Asian gangs unique is that they function in a closed culture that is often suspicious of and unwilling to cooperate with law enforcement. Gang activity and organized crime is deeply rooted in Asian culture and is often an accepted part of life and business. An example of this is that many Asian businesses consider paying "protection" to street gangs a normal business cost similar to paying the rent or the power bill.

Asian Gangs

26th Street Chinatown Crew
AK Boys
American Eagles
Asian Boy Crips
Asian Boys
Asian Empire
Asian Family
Asian Gangster Crips
Asian Gangsters
Asian Girls (Female)
Asian Killers
Asian North Side Crips
Asian Piru Bloods
Asian Posse

Asian Pride
Asian Ruthless Boys
Asian V Boys
Asian West Side Crips
Bad Boys
Black Dragons
Black Widows
Blood Red Dragons
Born To Kill (B.T.K.)
Boryokudan
Boston Red Dragon
Boys In Style (BIS)
Brighten Boys
Cambodian Crips
Cambodian Pride
Cheap Boys
Chinatown Rulers
Crazy Boy Clan
Crazy Oriental Crips
Criminal Asian Boys
Dai Huen Jai (Big Circle Boys)
Dangerous Nips
Dirty Punks
Dragon Family
East Side Oriental Boys
Easy Boys Gang
Evil Killers
Exotic Foreign Crip Creation
Flying Dragons
Forever Asian Boys
Fresh Oriental Bitches (female)
Fine Oriental Bitches (female)
Fuk Ching
Ghost Shadows
Green Dragons
Ha Tien Boys
Hip Sing
Hung Ching
Insane Green Piru
Jackson Street Boys
Junior Asian Pride
Junior Viet Pride
Lady Rascal Gangster
Laotian Boys
Laotian Cambodian Piru
Lao Pride Gangster
Little Asian Rascals
Little Green Pirus
Little Red Thugs
Laos Viet Connection
Local Boys
Local Town Crips
Lotus
Lue Boys
Master of Destruction
M'bros
Maung Thugs
Mongolian Boys Society
Natoma Boys
New Viet Gang
Nip Family
North Side Hip Sing
Oaktown Crips
Oriental Boys Society
Oriental Killer Boys
Oriental Lao Boys
Oriental Lazy Boys
Oriental Loko Boys
Oriental Mob Crips
Oriental Mon Boys
Oriental Play Boys
Oriental Rascals
Oriental Ruthless Boys (O.R.B.)
Oriental Street Boys
Oriental Street Girls
Oriental Troups
Original Crazy Boys
Pomona Girls
Redheads
Sacramento Bad Boys
Saigon Boys
Santa Anna Boys

Seattle Boys
Sons of Death
Sons of Samoa
Spider Boys
Street Killer Boys
Sworn Boys
The Lynx
Tiger Mafia
Tiny Locos
Tiny Loco Boys
Tiny Oriental Crips
Tiny Rascals
True Oriental Boys
Twenty Seven
United Bamboo Gang
Viet Boys
Viet Hung
Viet Pride
Viet Soldiers
Viet Thug Homies
Viet Hug Life
VTK
Wah Ching Gang
Wally Girls
West Philly Woo Boys
West Side Oriental Boys
Wolf Boys
Young Asian Boys
Young Oriental Gangsters

Asian Gang Tattoos, Symbols, Graffiti, and Marks

Dragon Claw
(Denotes Rank)

Born to Kill

Cigarette Burns
(See next page)

The Five Ts

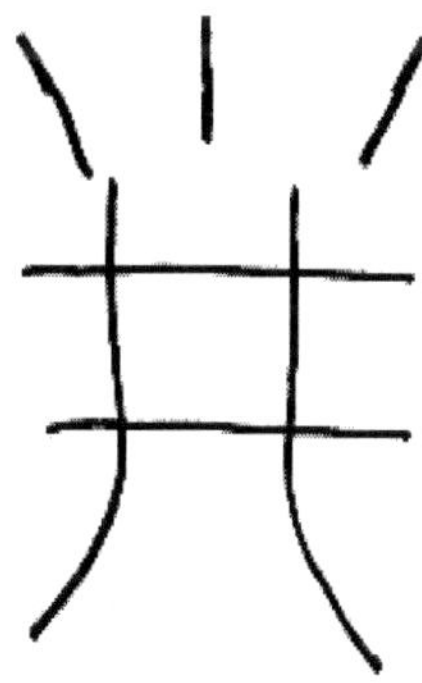
Triad
(Criminal & Legitimate)

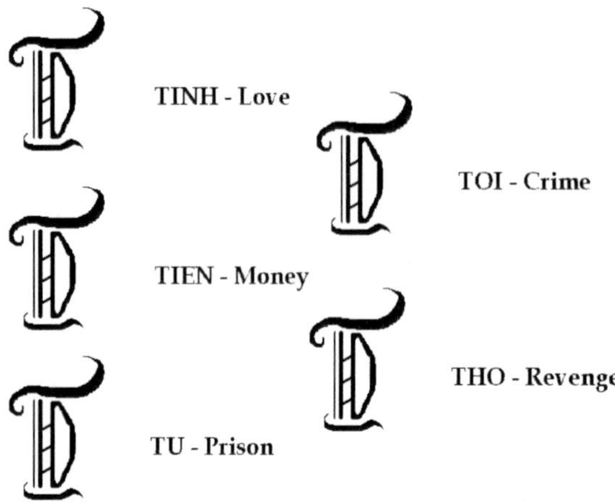

Note: Toi can also be translated as sin rather than crime.

Cigarette burns on the body are common among Asians gang members as a sign of courage and toughness. The following examples include a description of their meaning.

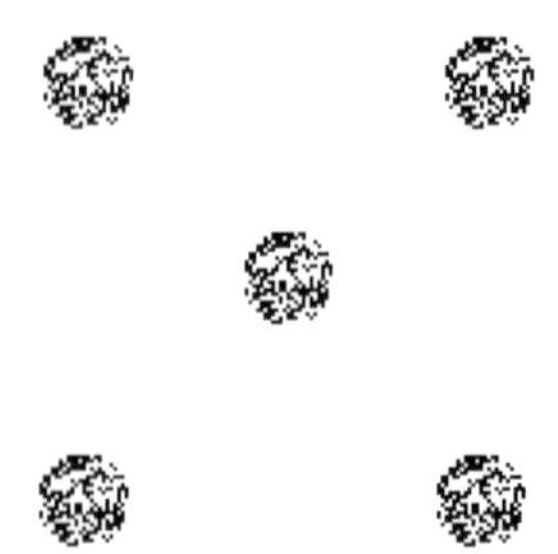

Five cigarette burns in the above pattern are generally found on Asian gang members of all kinds, as well as on Asians that are not members of gangs or STGs. Regardless, if the person bearing these marks is a gang or STG member or not, the marking represents the same thing, a group of friends or family members surrounding a fifth member or protecting the person in the middle.

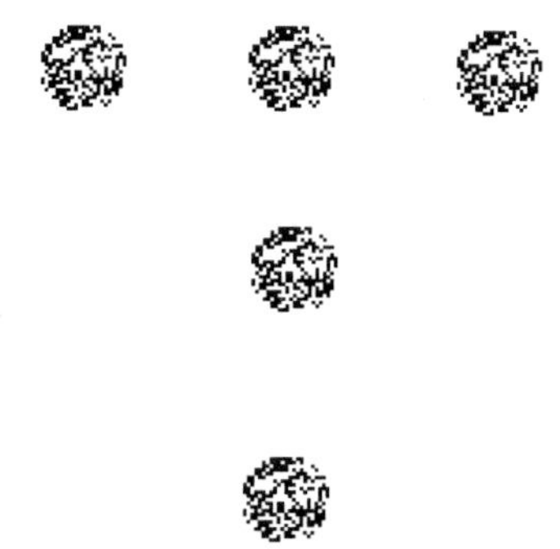

Five cigarette burns in this pattern are generally found on Asian gang and STG members. On occasion, this pattern can be found on Asians that are simply involved in criminal activity but are not gang or STG members. Each of the dots represents one of the Five Ts. The five Ts are Tinh (Love), Tien (Money), Tu (Prison), Toi (Crime), and Tho (Revenge).

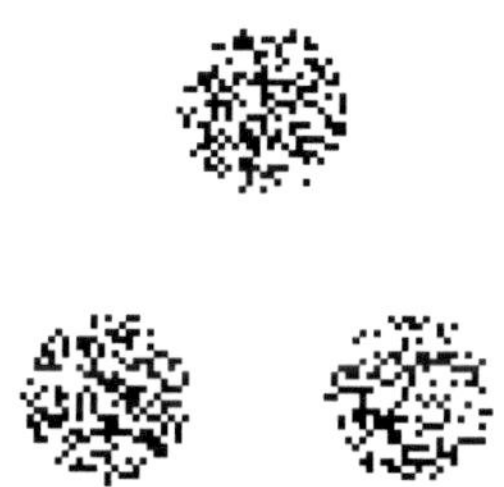

As with any other set of three dots, this set of burns represents the saying "My Crazy Life" or "A Life Lost." Although this saying originated within the Hispanic culture, this saying has crossed most cultural boundaries and is common among all gang and STG members either in the form of a tattoo or a cigarette burns.

Hierarchy (Triads and Tongs)

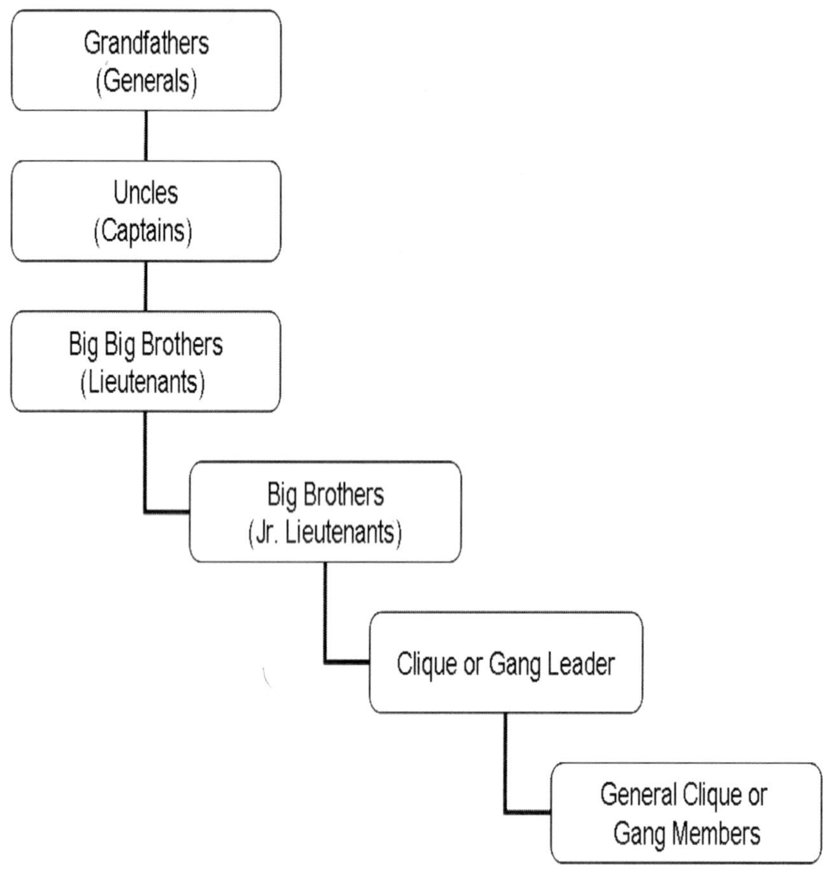

(Source: Officer Mel Cobb, Aurora Police Department, Aurora Colorado)

This hierarchy generally applies to Tongs and Triads regardless of their country of origin. Each country of origin has different words for each of these ranks, but their generalized meaning is as above and is consistent from one group to the next. The ranks provided in parentheses were added by the author to illustrate a rank structure in terms that are familiar to reader.

General Asian Street Gang Hierarchy

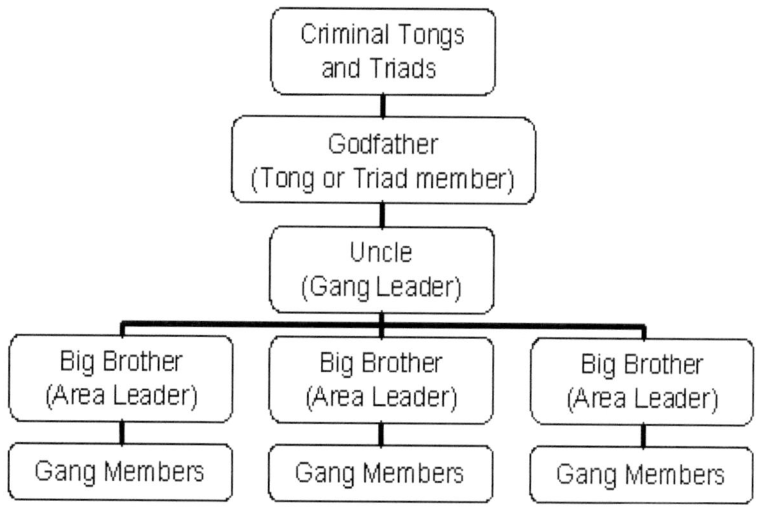

Understanding Asian Sir Names

1. **Vietnamese**

   Names are written: *Family (Last), Middle, then First.*

   Examples of Common Family Names:

   Nguyen, Pham, Chuong, Tran, and *Vo*

2. **Cambodian**

   Names are written: *Family (Last), Middle, then First.*

   Examples of Common Family Names:

   Kim, Kong, Neang, Som, and *Chea*

3. **Laotian**

Names are written: *First, then Family (Last).*

Examples of Common Family Names:

Bouphasiri, Nasirichampang, and *Khamphoukeo*

4. **Hmong**

Names are written: *Clan (Last), Middle, then First*

Examples of Common Clan Names:

Lee, Chang, Thao, Vang, and *Kong*

5. **Mein**

Names are written: *Family or Clan (Last), Middle, then First.*

Examples of Common Family and Clan Names:

Saepan, Saeyang, Saelee, Saephan, and *Saeturn*

Introduction

The Hispanic gang and STG category covers a wide variety of gangs and groups made up of individuals of Hispanic descent from throughout North and South America. Although many of these gangs and groups share a common Hispanic heritage, the truth is they hate each other for their minor differences, in some cases as much as White supremacy groups hate non-Whites. With this in mind, it is important to remember that a common Hispanic heritage does not guarantee a climate of cooperation between these gang and groups anymore then a shared African-American heritage guarantees cooperation between the Crips and the Bloods or the Gangster Disciples and the Vice Lords.

It is also important to note that Sureño 13–associated gangs show allegiance of varying degrees to the Mexican Mafia and Norteño 14 associated gangs show allegiance to La Nuestra Familia. The Mexican Mafia and La Nuestra Familia are the two largest Hispanic STGs/organized crime groups in the California prison system and have a long history of disruptive/criminal behavior as well as an international influence. The following information about Hispanic gangs and STGs represent the largest and most well-known Hispanic gangs and STGs in the country and in Colorado.

Mexican Mafia Sects

Mexican Mafia (Original, California, Southwest, and Mexico)
New Mexican Mafia (Arizona, Southwest, and Mexico)
New Mexican Mafia of Texas a.k.a. Mexikanemi (Texas, Southwest, and Mexico)
Old Mexican Mafia (Arizona, Southwest, and Mexico)

Note: The original Mexican Mafia was founded in California and is well established both in the California Department of Corrections and the Federal Bureau of Prisons. The New Mexican Mafia in Arizona, and the Mexikanemi in Texas, are spin off sects of the original Mexican Mafia. Although not considered outright rivals, there is constant tension between these three groups.

Mexican Mafia Tattoos, Marks, and Symbols

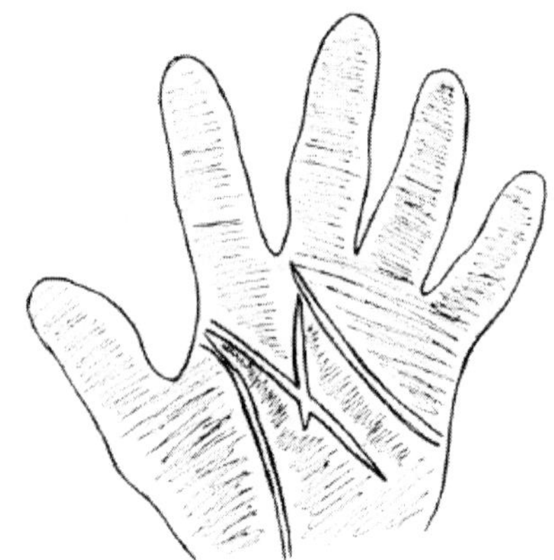

The Black Hand

Mexican Mafia

13

M

The History of the Mexican Mafia

THE MEXICAN MAFIA
"eMe"

Type of Gang:	Non-traditional
Founded:	1957
Founded by:	Luis "Huero" Flores in the Duel Vocational Institution
General racial makeup:	Mexican American
Main rivals:	Norteño 14 gangs, La Nuestra Familia, and the Black Guerilla Family

Major historical events:

1968—the "Shoe Wars" erupt in the California Department of Corrections, leading to the separation of street gangs into Sureño 13 and Norteño 14 groups.

1969—Joe Morgan becomes a member of the Mexican Mafia at age 40 and later becomes known as the "Godfather."

1970s—the Mexican Mafia gains control of the "Get Going Project" and the "Community Concern Cooperation," both groups are funded by State of California.

1960 – Present—the Mexican Mafia is targeted by law enforcement.

1960 – Present—the Mexican Mafia collects taxes on narcotics sales.

Mexican Mafia Hierarchy

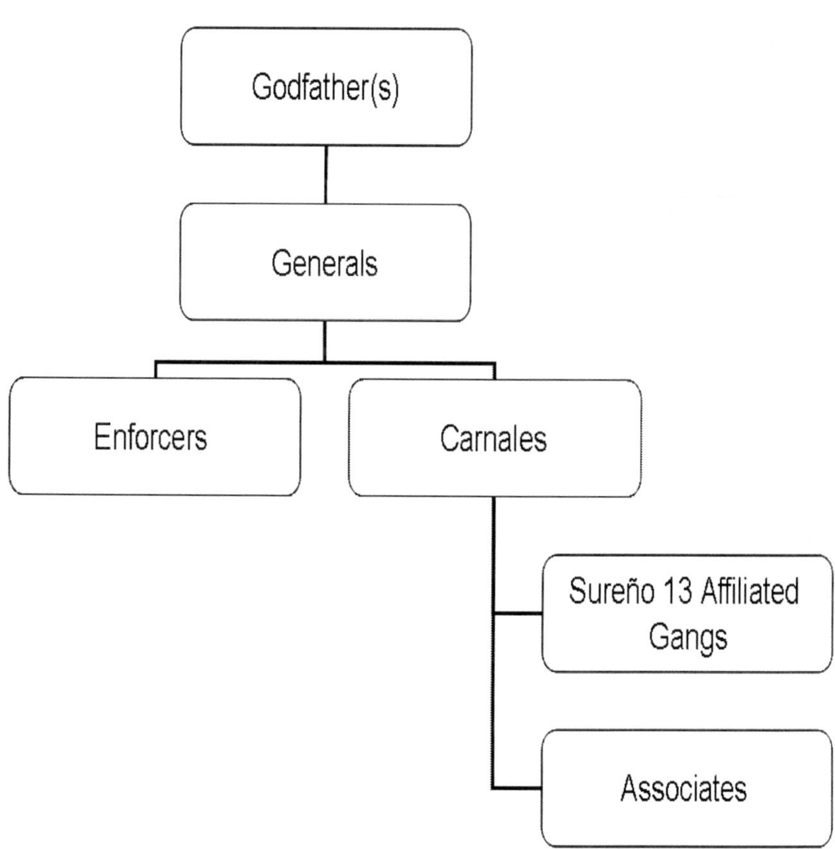

There is some controversy over the title of "Godfather." Some experts state that the only person to hold the rank of Godfather was Joe Morgan. Although his leadership position was filled after his death, it is believed the title of Godfather will never be bestowed on anyone out of respect for Joe Morgan. Other experts will tell you that the term Godfather refers to anyone with authority over "Generals." Also, it is important to remember that each prison has its own hierarchy that is responsible for activity that takes place in each prison. These prison hierarchies then answer to the overall leadership.

Mexican Mafia Drug Taxation

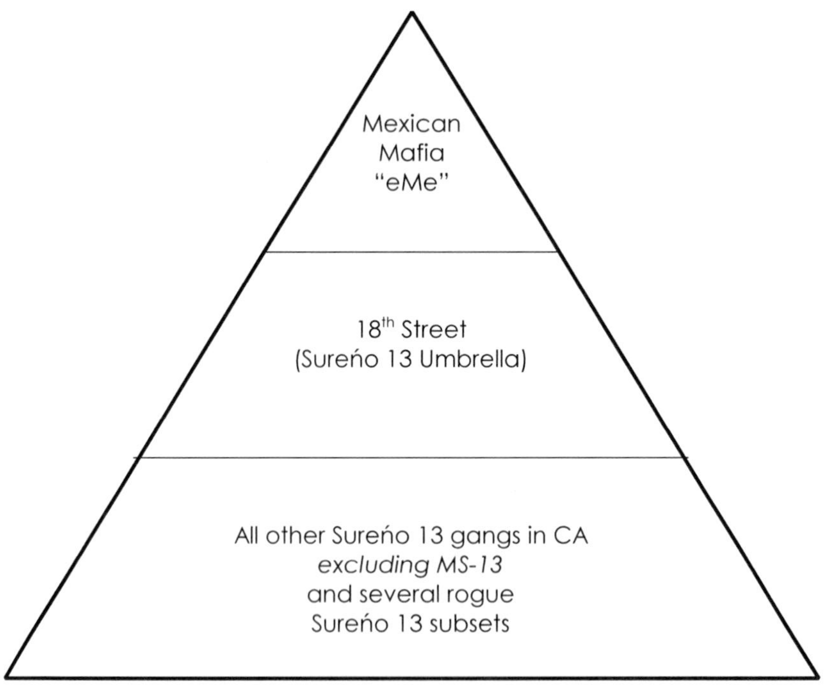

Through intimidation, tradition, and survival the Mexican Mafia collects a "tax" from the majority of the Sureño 13 gangs in the California area. The amount of the tax varies; this taxation does not appear to have extended past the California borders to non-California based Sureño 13 gangs. As an example, local Colorado Sureño 13 know little about the Mexican Mafia or their influence on the California narcotics trade. Understanding this is necessary to understanding the California gang culture, its influences on the U.S. gang culture, and the rivalry with the La Nuestra Familia and Norteño 14–based gangs.

Sureño 13 Affiliated Gangs

4th Flats
5th Street
7th and Broadway
7th Street
7/11 Locos
11th Street
14th Street Dukes
17th Street Tiny Locos
18th Street
18th Street (South Side)
18th Street (West Side)
18th Street Hynas (Female)
19th Street San Fran. MS13
20th Street
20th Street San Fran. MS13
22 Abriles Locos Salvatruchos
30th Street
38th Street
42nd Street Sureño 13
43rd Street
47th Street
54th
57th Street
60's MS13
64th Street Lokotes
106th
804 Locos
970 Outlaws
Acasio 13
Azusa 13
Adams Blvd
Adams Locos
Alsace Locos
Alveras Kings
Arizona Mara
Arizona Sur Gang
Assassins
Atwater 13
Avenues
Azusa 13
B. Street
Baby Gangster Sureños
Bandido Sureños
Barrio Centro 13
Barrio Diesiocho
Barrio Fallbrook Locos
Barrio Gangster
Barrio Hollywood 13
Barrio Libre 13
Barrio Locos 13
Barrio Locos (Female)
Barrio Los Padrinos
Barrio Negro
Barrio Pobre
Barrio South Side
Barrio Sur Trece
Basset Grande
Bebitos
Bell Gardens
Besamer Park Loco
Big Time Locos
Big Time Sureños
Biola
Block Boys
Blue Devils
Blue Side Villains
Blythe Street
Bolen Parque 13

Born Insane Crew
Brick City
Brick City Boys
Brown Crowd
Brown Crowd Babies
Brown Crowd Bandits
Brown Crowd Youngsters
Brown Magic Clica
Brown Nation
Brown Neighborhood
Brown Pride
Brown Town
Brown Town Mayan 13
Calle Locos
Canoga Parque
Carmelas Varrio Lokotes
Casa Blanca
Centro City Locos
Cerco Blanco 13
Chapines Treces
Chicano Gangster Bitchs
Chicos
Chiques 13
City Stoner 13
City Terrace X3
Coliseo Locos Salvatruchos
Colonia Chique
Coloni Oxnard
Colorado Craziest Chicanos
Columbia Lil Cycos
Compton Varrio Tee Flat
Corona 4th Street Assassins
Coronado Psychos MS13
Crazy Rider Sureño
Culver
Culver City
Cyclones
Cypress Avenues
Cypress Park
Daiblos
Dead End 13
Denver Mile High
Diamond Street
Dirty Ghetto Kriminals
Division Street
DM Gangsters
Downey Boys
Drew Street
Driver Side
Dukes
East Fax Locos Sureños
East Side 13
East Side Bakers
East Side Coxch
Eastlake
East Los
East Los Angels
East Side 13
East Side Long Beach
East Side Salvatruchos
East Side San Diego
East Side Santa Barbara 13
East Side Sureño
East Side Torrence
East Side Victorville
Easy Riders
Ever Green
El Monte 13
El Monte Flores
El Monte Hicks
Fichett Street
Fifth and Hill
Five Nine Four
Florencia 13
Ford Mara
Francis Locos Salvatruchos
Friar Street
Frogtown
F-Troop 13
Fuck Our Enemies
Fulton Street Loco
Gardena 13

Garatty Lomas
Geraghty
Ghetto Boys 13
Glassel Park
Glendale (18th St)
Grand View Locos
Harbor Area 13
Hardtimes 13
Harpy's
Harvard St Criminals
Hate Town Sureño
Hauser Blvd (18th St)
Hawthorne 13
Hazard
Hazard Grande
Heartless Killers
Highland Park 13
Hitman Posse (Florida)
Hollywood Gangsters
Hollywood Locos MS 13
Hoover Locos
Hopeless Killers
Hoyo Mara
Inglewood 13
Insane Boys
Island Bound Sureño
Judas 13
Juarez 13
Juaritos 13
Just a Dream Sureño 13
Kansas Street
K Dub
King Boulevard G'S
King Kobras
Krazy Ass Mexicans
Krazy Down Players
Krazy Town
KWS Southgate
La Gara
La Gran Familia
La Loma 13
La Primera
La Posada
La Puente 13
La Rana
La Victoria Locos
Laguna Park Vikings
Las Lomas
Latinos Never Stop
Lennox 13
Lil Crazy Sureño
Lil Criminals
Lil Cycos
Lil Lowks
Lil Pee-Wees
Lil Valley Locos
Lil Watts
Linda Vista
Little Counts
Little East Side
Little Valley
Little Valley Lokotes
Loced Out Criminals
Locos 13
Locos Sureño 13
Locos Sureño Town
Locos Vatos Town
Logan Heights (Varies)
Logan Heights Calie Treinta
Logan Heights Redtops
Loked Out Criminals
Loked Up Kriminals
Lomita Villages 70s
Lomitas Park Locos
Lonely South Side Chicanos
Longtown Creepers
Lonely SS Chicanos
Lopez Maravilla
Los Coyotes 13
Los Ochentas
Los Players
Lynwood Varrio Dukes

Malditos 13
Mara Salvatrucha 13
Maravilla
Marianna Maravilla
Marijuanos Mexicanos
Market Street Gang
Maywood (18th St)
Mexican Criminal Mafia
Mexican Locote
Mexican Pride Sureño
Mexican Sureño 13
Mexicano Molitos
Missions Bay 13
Midgets
Mobbing the Street Krew
Moon City Mafia
Monrovia
MS South Sac
MS 60's MS13
Niteowls
Normande Locos
North Side Redondo
Northwest Alabama
Nueva Trece
Nueva Sur
NSR 13
Ogden Trece
Old Gangster Sureño
Old Town N/S National City
Olden Boys
Only Mexican Clique
Ontario Black Angels
Ontario Varrio Sureño
Opal Street
Orange County Mafia
Orphan Pee-Wees High St
Out For Kash
Outlaws 13
Pacas 13
Pacas Flats
Paso Robles Boyz
Pacoima Sureño 13
Pacomima Criminals
Padrinos
Paradise Hills Locos
Paramount 13
Parkview Locos
Parkview MS 13
Pasadena Latin Kings
Peaceful Valley
Pee-Wees
Pee-Wee G's
Pico Locos
Pilo Street
Plant City
Playboys
Play Girl Sureñas (Female)
Palaza Vieja
Pomona (varies)
Pomona 12th Street
Pomona Shakeys
Ponchos Trece
Por Vida 13
Poserz 13
Primera Flats
Prima Loca 13 (Street)
Project Boys
Project Lokos
Puro Sureño 13
Puro Sureño Locos
Quinta Loma
R 13
Radford Street
Rancho Park
Rebels 13
Red Shield Boys
Red Steps
Redondo 13
Reseda 13
Rimpau
Riverside Locotes
Rockwood Street Locos 13

San Fer 13
San Gabriel Vallie Sureños
San Matas Sureño
San Street 13
Santa Fe Springs
Saqonaraa Varrio 13
Sea Side Locos
SGV Lomas
Shatto Park Locos
Shelltown 38th Street
Shelltown Gamma St Boys
Sharkies
Sherman 20th Street
Siete Shadow
Sir Galahad Criminals
Smiley Drive
South 1st
South 17th Street
South Park Local
South Side 13
South Side Bitches (Female)
South Side Chicanos 13
South Side Cliqua
South Side Denver Sureño
South Side Familia
South Side Locos
South Side Loonies
South Side Marijuaneros
South Side Montebello X3
South Side Players 13
South Side Raskals
South Side Riders
South Side Tokers
South Side Vatos
South Side Varrio Locos
South White Fence
Sox Los 13
Spida Clica
State Street Locos
Stoners 13
Sunnyvale Sur 13
Sur Crazy Ones
Sur North Side Mafia
Sur Town Locos
Sur Trece Brown Pride
Sur Trece Fredrick
Sur Wicked
Sureño Cholo
Sureño Por Vida
Sureño Trece Gangster
Sureño Trece Sisters
Sureño Life Style
Sureñas Locas (Female)
Sureñas Malditas (Female)
Sureñas Malditas Locos (Female)
Sureño Trece Sisters (Female)
Sur Side Loka 13
Temple Street
Tejas Sureño 13
Tejas Sureñas 13 (Female)
Tepas 13
The #1 Sureños
The Mob Crew
Tiny Diablos
Tiny Dukes
Tiny Locos
Tiny Loks Sureño 13
Tiny Malditos
Tiny Winos
Tokerstown 13
Toonerville Gangsters
Tortilla Flats
Townsmen Gang
Trece Controla
Trece Tokers
Tres Hate Town
Vagos Sureño 13
Valley (18th Street)
Valmont Loco Trece
Vail Street
Van Nuys 13

Varrio 42 Lil Criminals
Varrio Arta
Varrio Bellflower Locos
Varrio Brick City Sureño
Varrio Chino Sinners Gang
Varrio Encanto Locos
Varrio Grape Street
Varrio Lomas
Varrio Mafia Treces
Varrio Nuevo X3
Varrio Sureño Locos
Varrio Sureño Town
Varrio Sureño Treces
Varrio Vista Rifia
Varrio Mischief Sur 13
Varrio Norwlk
Varrio Nuevo Estrada
Varrio Spring Valley Lokos
Varrio Sureños Lokotes
Varrio Tres
Vatos Locos
Vaughn Street
Venice 13
Verdugo
Vineland Boys 13
Wall Street
Watts Varrio Grape
Western Locos
West Oakland 17th Street
West Side Locos
West Side Locotes
West Longos
West Side Long Beach
West Side Playboys Wanderers
West Side Rubidoux Play Girls 13
West Side Sureños
West Side Via Loco
Westborough Park
White Fence
Wicked Ass Sureños
Wicked Lokos
Wicked Side 35th Street
Wicked South Locos 13
Wilmas Street
Wilmer Street Locos
Winter Gardens
Yolo County Sureño
Young Crazy Criminals
Young Crowd
Young Mexican Gangsters

Sureño 13 Tattoo, Symbols, Graffiti, and Marks

13

Mexican Mafia

Area Code for Southern California

M

Mara Salvaturcha 13

Mara Salvaturcha (13)

Azteca Shield

The History of Sureño 13 and Other Associated Gangs

SUREÑO 13
SUR 13

Type of Gang: Traditional
Founded: 1960s
Founded by: Street gangs in Southern California supporting the criminal enterprise headed by the Mexican Mafia (an alliance).
General racial makeup: Mexican Americans
Main rivals: Norteño 14 street gangs and La Nuestra Familia.
Major historical events:

1968—participated in the "Shoe Wars" in the California Department of Corrections.

Adopted the 13 as a sign of respect to the Mexican Mafia (the 13th letter of the alphabet is "M," which stands for "eMe").

Late 1960s until present—Sureño 13 gangs are targeted by law enforcement.

MARA SALVATRUCHA
"MS," "MS-13"

Type of Gang: Traditional

Founded: 1980s

Founded by: Refuges who were former members of the La Mara (a criminal organization in El Salvador) or of the Farabundo Mart or the National Liberation Front, which is better known as FMNL (a guerrilla army in El Salvador) in Ramparts, California

General racial makeup: El Salvadorians, South Americans, and Hispanics

Main rivals: Non-Sureño 13–based gangs

Major historical events:

1980s—Guerrilla fighters and refugees flee El Salvador and settle in California and along the East Coast in the United States.

1980s—MS was at war with the Mexican Mafia.

Late 1980s – early 1990s—The Mexican Mafia and the MS form an alliance. MS becomes known as MS-13

In the 1980s—MS-13 members are targeted by law enforcement and death squads (La Sombra Negra or the Black Shadow) if they are deported to El Salvador.

1990s—MS-13 begins to allow non-Salvadorian membership

2006—National Geographic creates a documentary calling MS-13 "The Most Dangerous Gang." The FBI begins to crack down on the MS-13 nationwide.

2008 – 2010—MS reportedly dropping the number 13 from its name to show it separation from the Mexican Mafia.

La Nuestra Familia Tattoos, Marks and Symbols

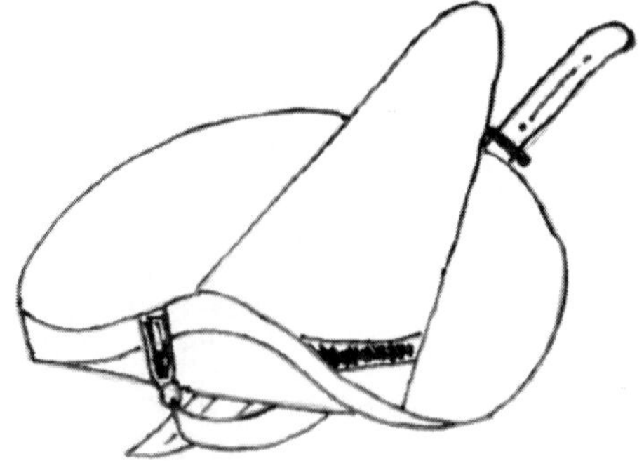

The Sombrero and Dagger

Norte
North or Norteño

14
N

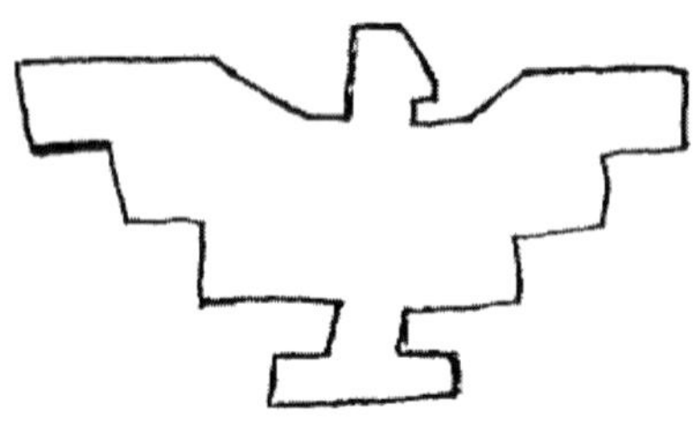

Helga Bird

La Nuestra Familia

The History of La Nuestra Familia

LA NUESTRA FAMILIA
"eNe"

Type of Gang: Non-traditional

Founded: Mid 1960s

Founded by: Gonzalo Hernandez and other inmates seeking protection from "eMe."

General racial makeup: Rural Mexican Americans

Main rivals: Sureño 13 gangs, the Mexican Mafia, and the Aryan Brotherhood

Major historical events:

Mid to late 1960—Gonzalo Hernandez organizes La Nuestra Familia.

1968—the "Shoe Wars" erupt in the California Department of Corrections leading to the separation of street gangs into Sureño 13 and Norteño 14.

Late 1960s – Present—the La Nuestra Familia is targeted by law enforcement.

Late 1960s – Present—the La Nuestra Familia collects taxes from narcotics sales.

Late 1990s—Robert Gratton is paroled from prison and creates North Star Records.

Late 1990s—North Star Records acts as a front for La Nuestra Familia.

2001—the "Black Widow" indictments are filed against La Nuestra Familia with Robert Gratton as the main witness. After conviction of key members of the La Nuestra Familia, leadership is moved to Federal Prisons throughout the United States.

La Nuestra Familia

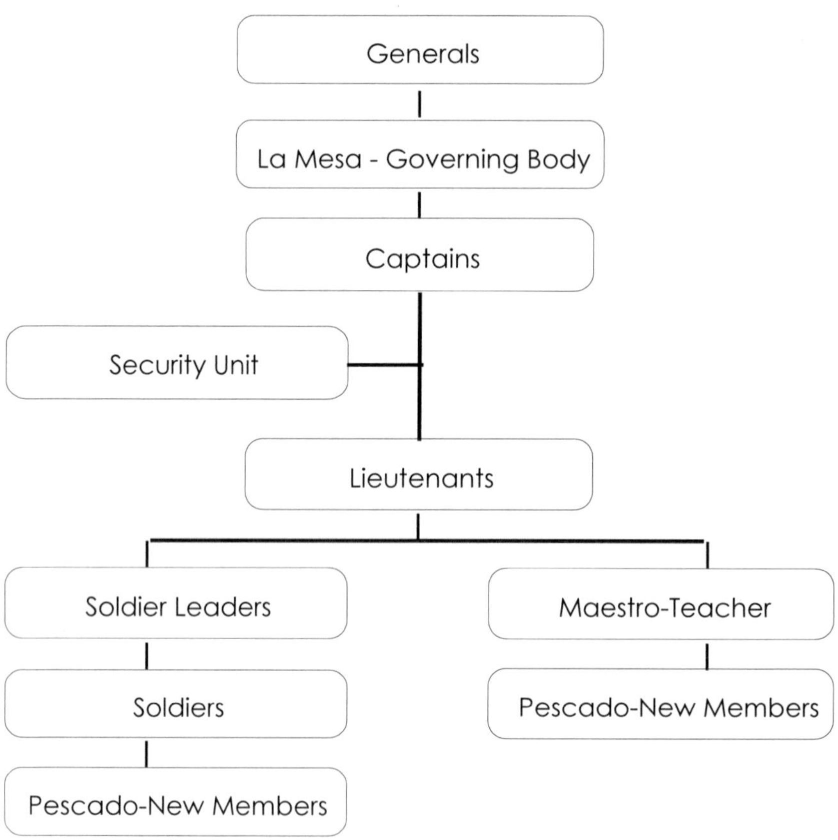

Norteño 14–affiliated gangs take their directions from La Nuestra Familia in the same manner that Sureño 13 gangs take directions from the Mexican Mafia. Also, new members of La Nuestra Familia are generally recruited from the ranks of the Norteño 14 in the same manner that the Mexican Mafia recruits from the ranks of the Sureño 13.

Norteño 14 Affiliated Gangs

25th St. Norte
10th St. Norte
14th St. Norte
19th and Mission
21st St. Norte
500 Block
1100 Block Mobsters
2 FC
21st
22nd and Mission
24th and Mission
4th Street Barrio Small Town
Acorns
Avenal Varrio Lomas
Barrio Franklin Boys
Barrio Mas Locos
Barrio Pachuco
Barrio Hollis Territory
Bay Road
Bella Vista Park
Broderick Boys
Brown Pride
Brown Street Norte
Bryant Street Locotes
Bull Dogs
C Street
Capital Park Norteño
Cárdenas Mafia 14
Central
Centre Valley
Chankla Catore 14
Chi-Town Two Six Nation
City Hall Watson
Clantones 14
Clown Boys
Coalinga Norte
Cold Blooded Gangsters
Corcoran Norte
Crazy Girl Norteñas 14 (Female)
Crazy Lil Norteñas (Female)
Cypress Park Locos
Daily City Players
Daly City Locos
Darkroom Familia
Dead End Locos
Del Paso Heights
Diablo Park
Diablos Viejo
Diamond Street
Dirty 30's
Don't Give A Fuck
East 7th Street
East Las Casitas
East Palo Alto Locos 14
East Side
East Side Casitas
East Side Daly City
East Side Gilas
East Side Mod
East Side Palmas 14
East Side Hood
East Side Oakland
East Side San Jose
East Side Sharks
East Side Stockton
El Hoyo Palmas
Espanto Flats
F-14
Fair Oaks
Familia De Norte
Familia Varrio Loco
Firegaugk Norteño
Fog Town
Freemont Street Norte
Fresno Boys Norteño
Garden Block

Greeley XIV
Grinfas Tiny Locos
Hanford Home Gardens
Hanford South Side
Hayward Catorea 14
Huron Norteño
Kettleman Norteño
Killer Sharks
King City 14
La Krazy Criminals 14 (Female)
La Raza
Las Ninas Apestosas
Latina Ladies Del Norte
Liberal Kansas Norte
Lil Decoto Gangster
Lil Town Mission
Little Chicka Norteñas 14 (Female)
Little Mexican Gangsters
Little Varrio Norte
Loco North Side
Los Latinos Loc
Los Projectos Norteño
Los Vatos Desmadrosos 19th Street
Lough Bro Locos
Mendota Norteño
Merced Ghetto Boys
Milpais Varrio Primida
Newark Norteños
No Face Killer
Norteño Por Vida
North Bay Norteños
N/S Assassins
N/S Esterllas
N/S Hayword A Street
N/S Locos
N/S Lokos 14
N/S Gonza
N/S Norteños
N/S Villains
Northern Brother Los
North Boy Gangsters
North Star Soldiers
Oakland 38th Street
Oak Park
Original Loco Boys
Orland Northern Warriors
Our Dedicated Norteños
Out Side Posse
Palmas
Palmetto Boys
Park Side 14
Parkway Locos
Penta Vadio Norteño
Quience
Ralston Roll'n Gangsters
Red Rag Gang
Richmond Barrio Loco 14
Roosevelt Park Locos
Sac Street
Salinas East Market
San Joaquin Norteño
Sanger Norteño
Santa Rosa Norteños
Saudcedas De Varrio
Linda Rifas 14
Scrap Killa
Selma Norteño
Shark City Locos
Soledad Vato Locos
Sonoma Norteños
South Hayward Norte
South Hayword FP Hood
South Park Norte
South Side Lunatics 14
SS Stockton
Tiny Norteño Locos
Tracy Northern Warriors
Tulare County
Turlock

Varrio 12th Street
Varrio Bloody Waters
Varrio Campo Vida 21
Varrio Central Vallejo 14
Varrio Centro Fairlas
Varrio Centro Lodi
Varrio Centro Sacra
Varrio Chico London
Varrio Chico Norte
  Youngsters
Varrio Diamonds
Varrio East Hill
Varrio East Side
Varrio Franklin Blvd.
Varro Freeport Norteños
Varrio Garden Land
Varrio Gardens
Varrio Ghost Towns
Varrio Grande Deceto
Varrio Grinfas Norte
Varrio Hamilton City Loco
Varrio Horseshoe
Varrio Meadow Fair
Varrio Morgan Lomas
Varrio Norte Fremont
Varrio Norte Pride
Varrio North Side
Varrio North Town
Varrio Pine Canyon
Varrio Pinedale Norte
Varrio Santa Rosa
Varrio South East
Varrio South Park
Varrio Underwood Reales
  Vatos Locos
Varrio Locos Latinos
Village Boys
Village Drive
Village Way Locos
West 20th Street
West Berkeley 510 Norte
W/S Firebaugh Norte
W/S Berkeley
W/S Fresno
W/S Merced
W/S Mob
W/S San Mateo
W/S San Mateo Norte
Wino Park Locos
York Street Mob
Young Newark Locos
Yuba City Notra Locos
Zapata Park 14

Norteño 14 Tattoo, Symbols, Graffiti, and Marks

Norteño
Norteño 14

NOR
Norteño

Norte
Norteño or North

14
N

XIV
14

Sureño 13 Killer

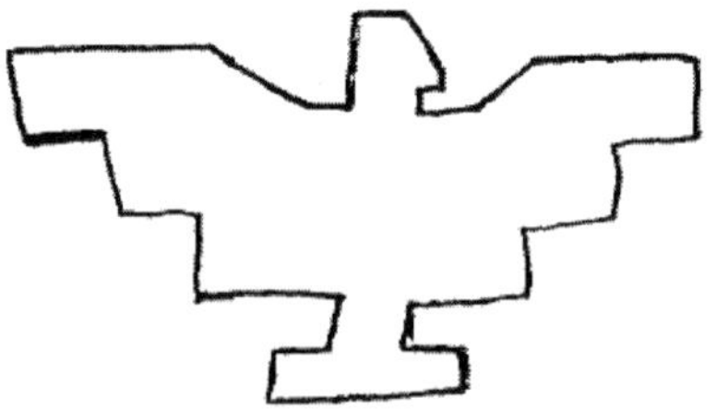
Helga Bird

La Nuestra Familia

The History of Norteño 14

NORTEÑO 14
NOR 14

Type of Gang:	Traditional
Founded:	1960s
Founded by:	Street gangs in Northern California supporting the criminal enterprise headed by the La Nuestra Familia (an alliance)
General racial makeup:	Mexican Americans
Main rivals:	Sureño 13 street gangs and the Mexican Mafia.

Major historical events:

1968—participated in the "Shoe Wars" in the California Department of Corrections.

Adopted the 14 as a sign of respect to the La Nuestra Familia (the 14th letter of the alphabet is "N" which stands for "eNe").

Late 1960s – present—Norteño 14 gangs are targeted by law enforcement.

Sureño 13 and Norteño 14 Division of California

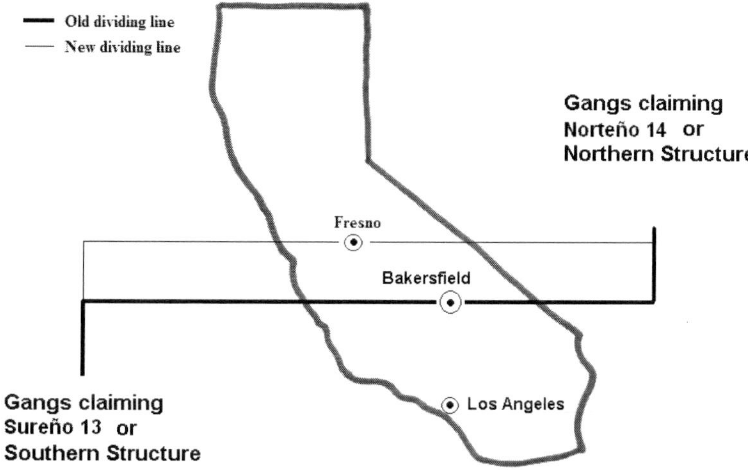

Traditionally, the dividing line between Norteño 14 and Sureño 13 dominated areas in California was Bakersfield. Over the last decade the dividing line has pushed north to approximately Fresno with the migration of Sureño 13 gangs into Northern California.

Tango Blast Cliques / Gangs

ATX/LA (Austin, Texas)
Chucos (El Paso, Texas)
Corpitos (Corpus Christie, Texas)
D-Town (Dallas, Texas)
Foros/Furitos (Fort Worth, Texas)
Orejones (San Antonio, Texas)
Puro Tango Blast
Puro West / Wesos (West, Texas)
Tango Blast
Screwtown (Houston, Texas)
Vallucos (Rio Grande Valley, Texas)

Tango Blast Tattoo, Symbols, Graffiti and Marks

Tango
Tango Blast

Blast
Tango Blast

713
Texas Area Code

214
Texas Area Code

Houstone
Tango Blast Clique

A-Town
Tango Blast Clique

Foritos
Tango Blast Clique

Dallas, Texas Star

Houston, Texas Star

16	**20**	**2**
P= Puro	T =Tango	B= Blast

Screwton

Tango Blast Clique

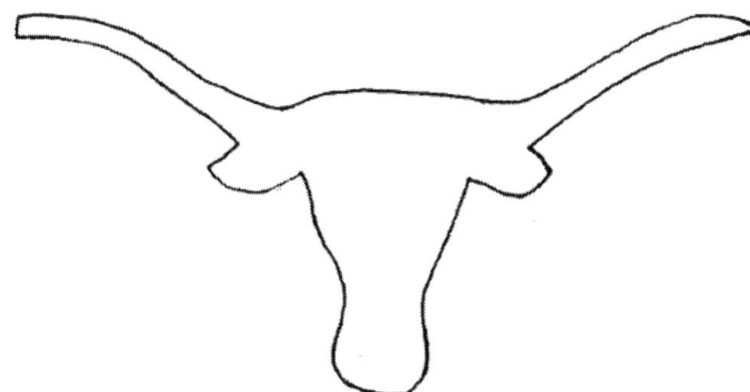

Texas Long Horn Steer

State of Texas

Tango Blast Gang Hierarchy

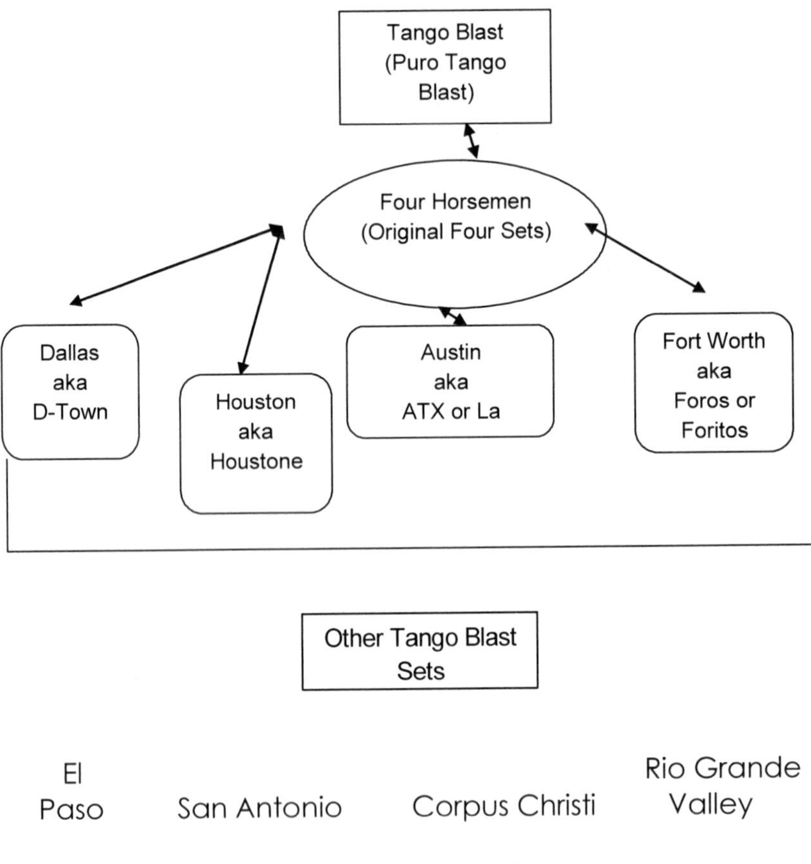

There is no known hierarchy within each set, city, or group claiming to be Tango Blast. Members from each city or area refer to themselves by "city of origin" and as a whole as Tango Blast. Individuals seeking membership in Tango Blast must have served prison sentences to obtain membership. Tango Blast is also unique in the fact that they do not require a "beat in" for initiation in the gang.

Barrio Azteca Tattoos, Symbols, Graffiti, and Marks

Feather Plumes
Containing 21 feathers
with 2 and 1 at the top.
(See Below)

Trust None
(Trust 2
One)

Feathers denote
rank
(See following page)

21

Stands for
B.A.

915

Area Code of
El Paso

EPT

El Paso, Texas

Azteca

Azteca

B.A.

Barrio Azteca

Barrio Azteca Rank Symbols

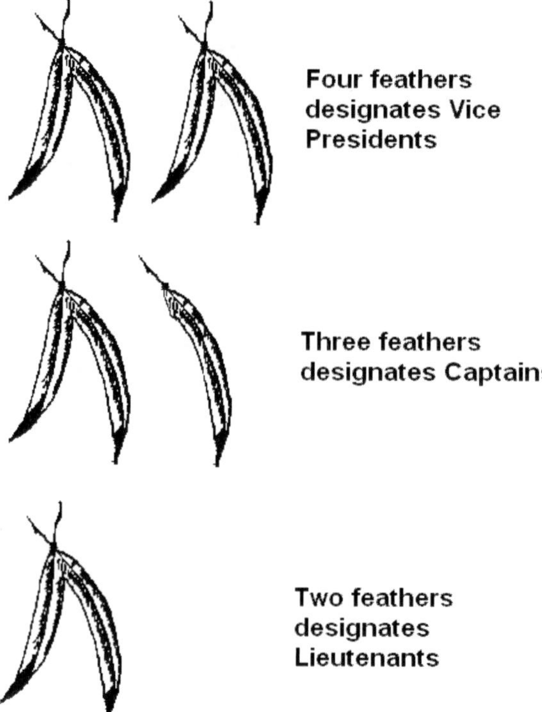

Feather plumes appear in many different configurations; however, it is the number of feathers that is important rather than their configuration. For example, twenty-one feathers in a plume signify the numbers 2 and 1, which stands for BA or Barrio Azteca. Two feathers sticking out of a plume followed by one feather sticking out of a plume also represent the numbers 2 and 1 or BA.

Barrio Azteca Hierarchy
The History of the Barrio Azteca

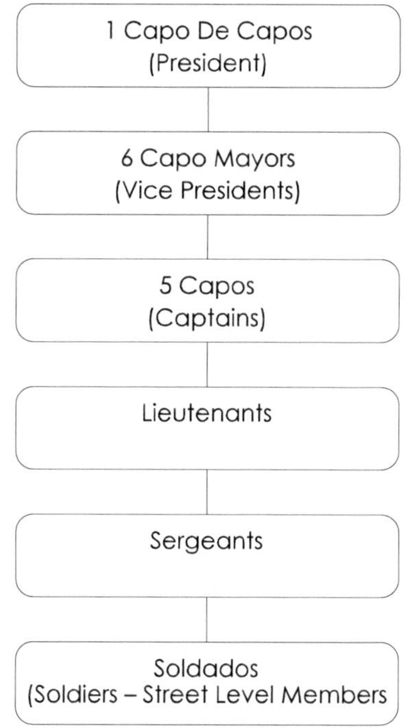

THE BARRIO AZTECA
"BAs"

Type of Gang: Non-traditional

Founded: 1986

Founded by: George Butes a member of the Mestizo, and four brothers, Benjamin, David, Francisco, and Pedro Acosta in the Texas Department of Corrections

General racial makeup: Hispanic

Main rivals: Aryan Brotherhood of Texas and the Texas Syndicate

Major historical events:
Signed a peace accord in 1997 with the Mexikanemi

One of the key facts that sets the BAs apart from other prison gangs is they do not allow their members to return to their original street gangs upon their release from a correctional facility. Once a gang member becomes a BA, he is supposed to renounce his claim to any other gang or group; however, members are allowed to use their old gangs and contacts to carry out BA-related criminal activity and business. While this fact sets them apart, the BA is much like larger prison gangs and STGs in the way they operate, even though they are much smaller in over all numbers. Examples of this can be found in the way the BA governs themselves and taxes the narcotic transactions of other gangs.

Paisa Tattoos, Symbols, Graffiti, and Marks

100% Paisa

Pure Countrymen

MADE IN

MEXICO

Made in Mexico
(Heche en Mexico)

100% Paisano

Pure Countrymen

Hecho en Mexico

Made in Mexico

Mexicano 100%

100% Mexican

16

Stand for the letter "P" or Paisa

Represents the Number 16

Paisa Hierarchy

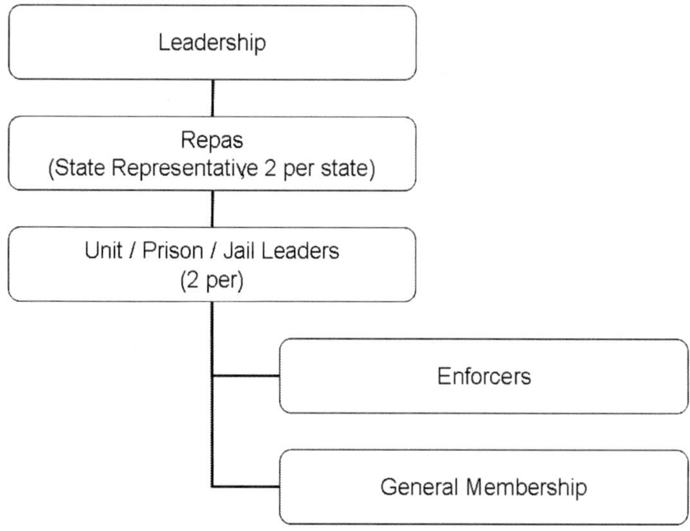

Texas Syndicate Tattoos, Symbols, Graffiti, and Marks

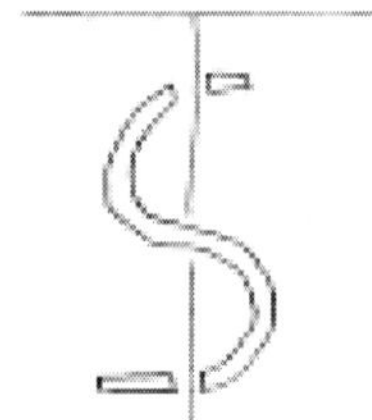

TS: Texas Syndicate

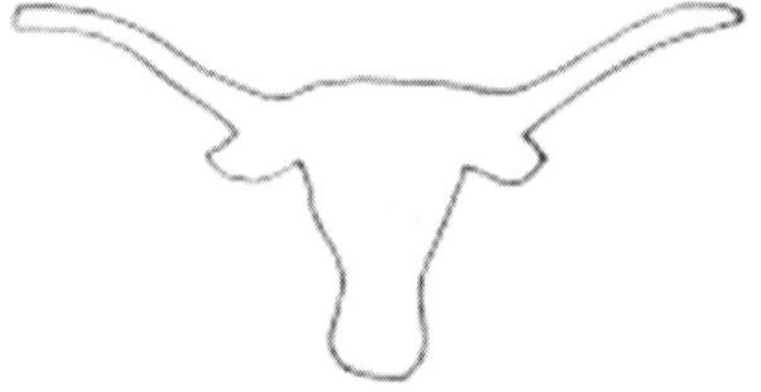

Texas Longhorn

State of Texas

Texas Syndicate Hierarchy

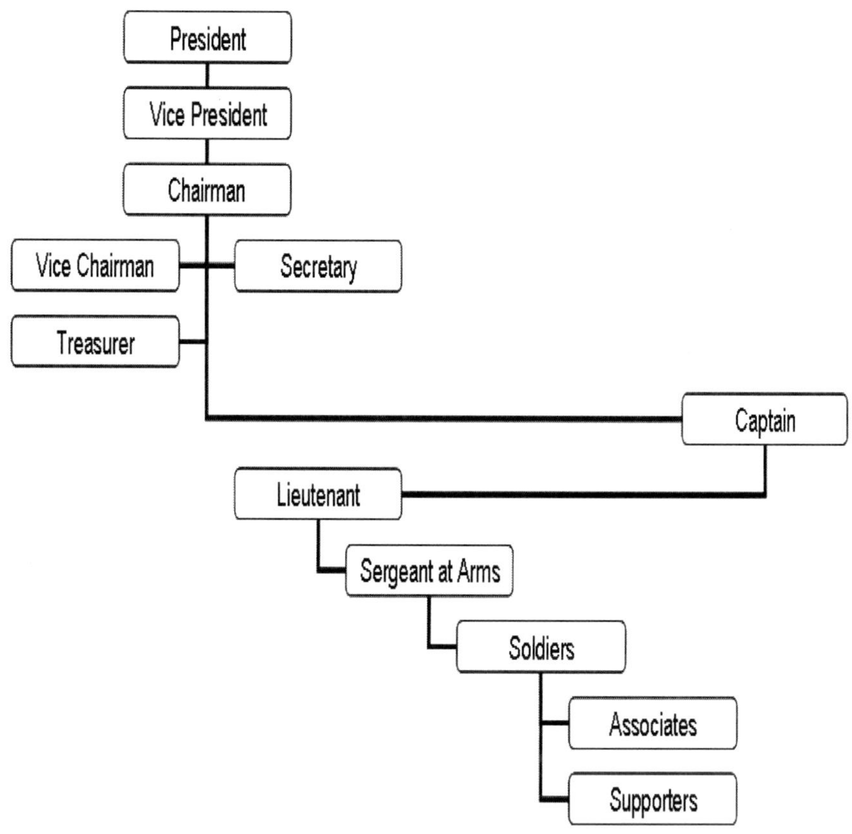

Gallant Knight Insane Sets

West Side Gallant Knights Insane, a.k.a., West Side GKI
(Original Set, Denver Colorado)
North Side Gallant Knights Insane, a.k.a., North Side GKI
(Newest set, North Denver Metro Area, Colorado)

Gallant Knights Insane Tattoo, Symbols, Graffiti and Marks

West 9th Avenue

Inca Boy Killer

G's Up

Gallant Knights Insane

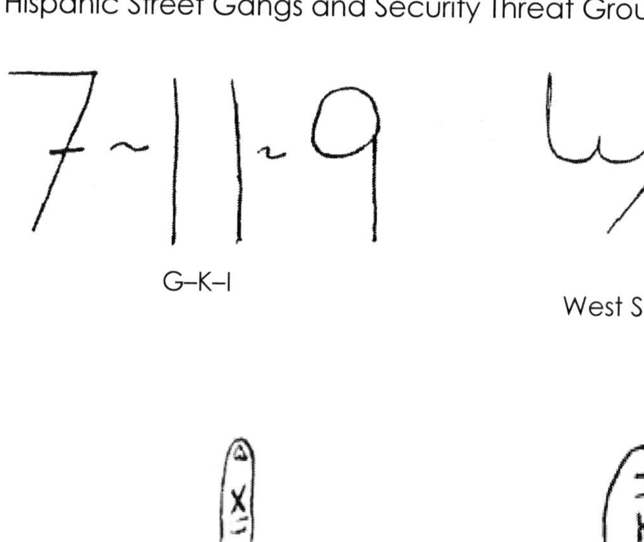

G–K–I

West Side

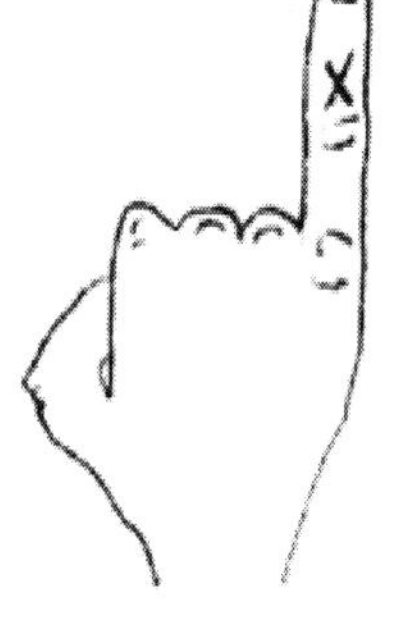

Inca Boy Killer

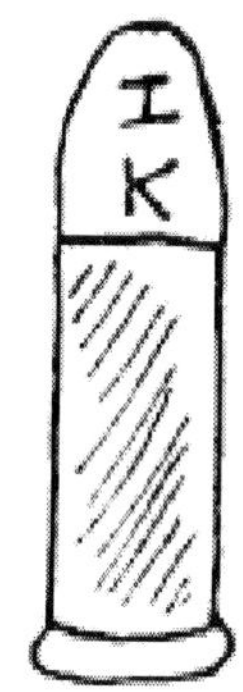

Inca Boy Killer

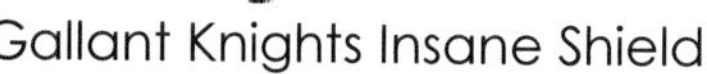

Gallant Knights Insane Shield

Gallant Knight

Gallant Knight Insane History

GALLANT KNIGHTS INSANE
"GKI"

Type of Gang: Traditional

Founded: Late 1980s

Founded by: Tom "Ninja" Cervantez, Mike "Phyco" Valenzuela, Andrew "Ox" Gutierrez, Eddie "Crazy Man" Munoz, Jimmy "Jimbo" Valenzuela, Joe "Cartwright" Montoya, and Philip "Phi Dog" Martinez

General racial makeup: Hispanic

Main rivals: Sureño 13, Norteño 14, Inca Boys, and other gangs

Main historical events:

1980–1990—Massive growth of GKI on the West Side of Denver, Co.

1990–2000—Created large drug networks and established connection to Mexican Cartels. Took control of Hispanic gang activity in the Colorado Department of Corrections.

2000–Present—Battling with Sureño 13 associated gangs to maintain control of gang activity in the Colorado Department of Corrections. Spread throughout the Denver Metro Area. Leadership of the gang is in disputed.

2006—GKI gang members were indicted under both R.I.C.C.O. and C.O.C.C.A.

Gallant Knight Insane Hierarchy

(Possible Chain of Command 2008)

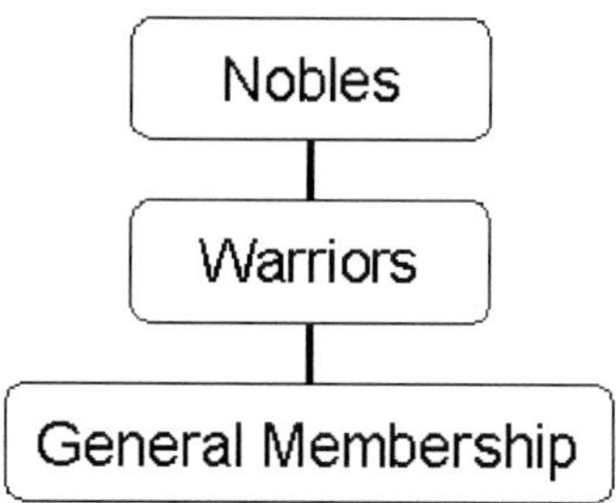

This "Chain of Command" for the Gallant Knights Insane (GKI) street gang was discovered in the Colorado Department of Corrections in 2008. At the time this documentation was discovered, the GKI were still reeling from Federal and State Organized Crime indictments. At the time of this discovery, the GKI was in the process of attempting to re-organize the gang to reestablish themselves in the criminal culture.

North Side Mafia Tattoo Symbols, Graffiti, and Marks

NSM Greeting

North Side Mafia

Sureño Killer

PURO

Pure NSM

14-19-13

N-S-M

Quig Newton Projects

Gorilla

Mafia

Mafia

14

N

North Side Mafia History

THE NORTH SIDE MAFIA
"NSM"

Type of Gang:	Traditional
Founded:	Mid to late 1980s
Founded by:	Juan Kuna and members of the 38th Street Specials, 44th Street Conquistadors, and the North Side Mojados
General racial makeup:	Hispanic
Main rivals:	Sureño 13–associated gangs

Major historical events:

Late 1980s—develop ties to Mexican Drug Cartels.

Early 1990s—ongoing turf battles with rival gangs to include the Gallant Knights Insane.

Mid to late 1990s—huge increase in Sureño 13 gangs in the Denver Metro Area create pressure on the NSM leading to an alliance with the Gallant Knights Insane.

2000s—battle Sureño 13 gangs for power in the Department of Corrections as well as on the street.

North Side Mafia Hierarchy

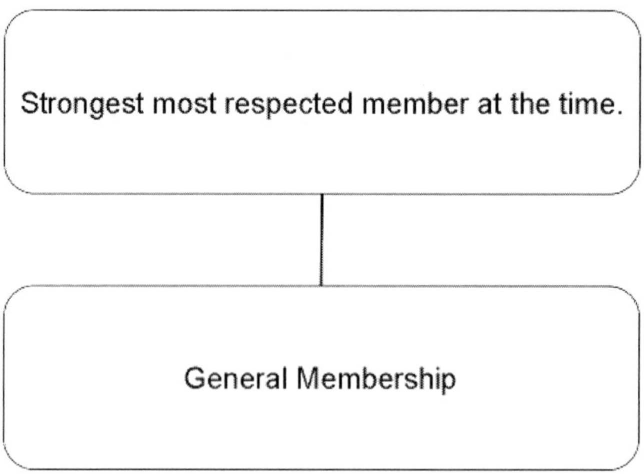

The North Side Mafia has no real structured leadership. The strongest or most respected leader present at the time will generally make decisions for the larger group.

Other Hispanic Gang Hierarchies

La Gran Familia Hierarchy

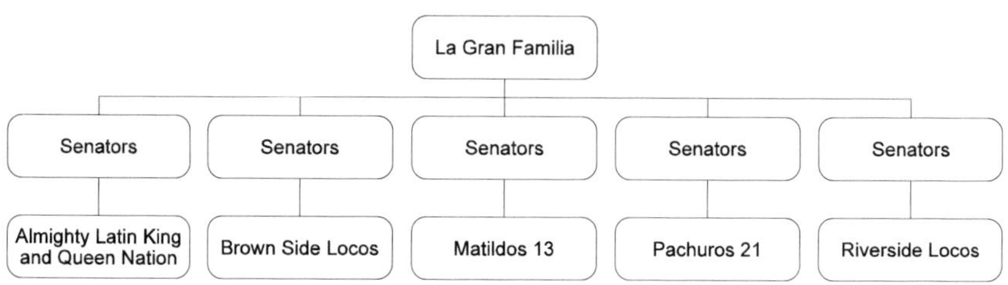

Founded in Atlanta, Georgia 1990.

Los Solidos Hierarchy

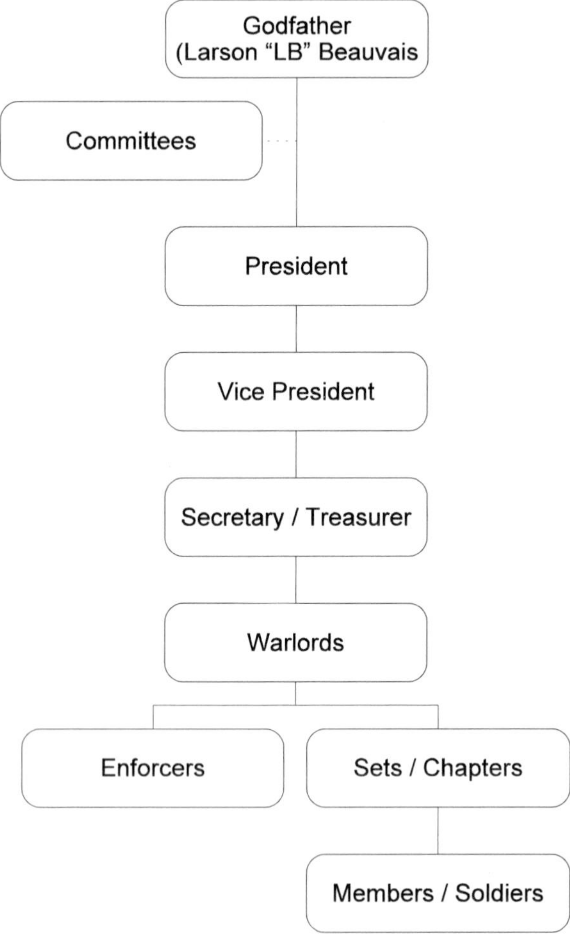

Mexican Criminal Organization

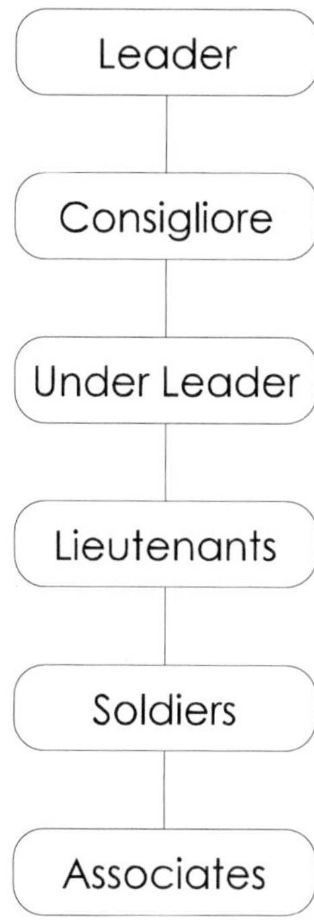

The Mexican Criminal Organization hierarchy was found in the cell of a jailed inmate. Although little is known about MCO by the author, it is worth including as another example of a gang hierarchy.

The History of the La Gran Familia

LA GRAN FAMILIA

Type of Gang:	Organized Crime
Founded:	Late 1980s early 1990
Founded by:	An alliance of five gangs: the Almighty Latin King and Queen Nation, Brown Side Locos, Maltidos 13, Pachucos 21, and the Riverside Locos in Atlanta, Georgia
General racial makeup:	Hispanic.
Main rivals:	Gangs not affiliated with La Gran Familia

Main historical events:

2002—fifty-one members indicted under R.I.C.C.O.

Other Hispanic Gang Histories

Los Solidos

Type of Gang:	Traditional
Founded:	Late 1980s early 1990
Founded by:	Larson (LB) Beauvais, Connecticut Correctional Facilities
General racial makeup:	Hispanic
Main rivals:	The Almighty Latin King and Queen Nation.

Main historical events:

2005—Operation Willi Riders led by the Drug Enforcement Administration ends with the indictment of fifty members of Los Solidos.

Border Brothers Expansion and Migration

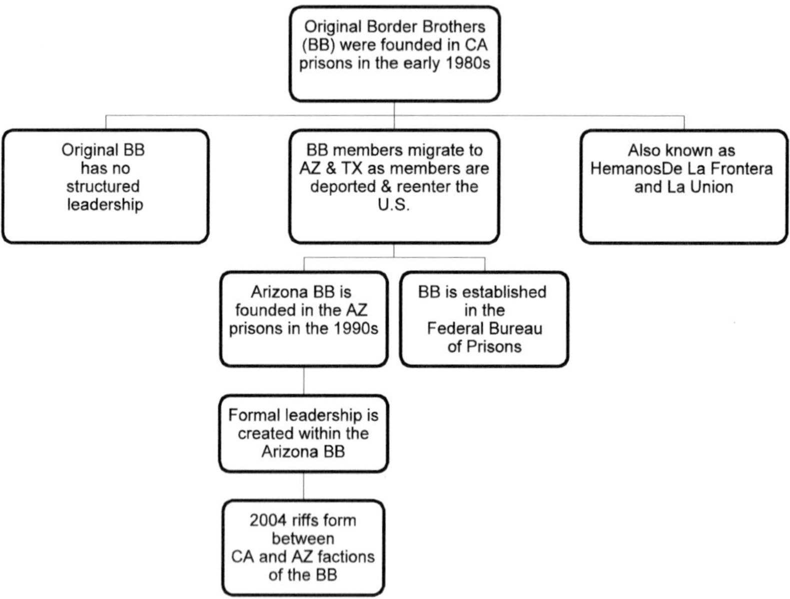

Source: Ramon Suarez CCA and Interviews with B.B. Members

Other Hispanic Gang Symbols, Graffiti, Marks, and Tattoos

Hermandad De Pistoleros Latinos Tattoo, Symbols, Graffiti, and Marks

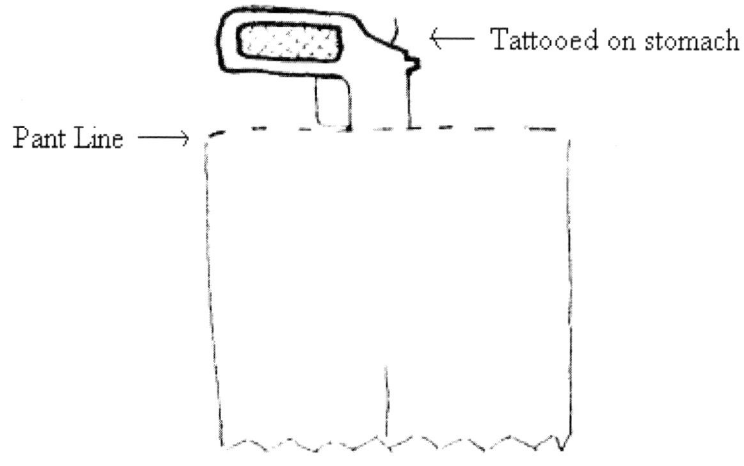

Pistol Abdomen Tattoo

HPL

Border Brother Tattoo, Symbols, Graffiti, and Marks

Border Brothers

BB

Border Brothers

Introduction

There is often a debate between people as to the true nature of motorcycle clubs/gangs. Some people believe that motorcycle clubs/gangs do not possess an immediate threat to the community or to law enforcement. On the other hand there are those that feel motorcycle clubs/gangs possess nothing less then an immediate threat to the community and law enforcement and, therefore, should be treated like any other organized criminal group.

The answer to this long running debate is "Yes." There are motorcycle gangs/clubs that possess an immediate threat to the community and to law enforcement (1% and puppet clubs) and those that do not (riding clubs and associations). The following information pertains to 1% (see glossary for definition) or Outlaw Motorcycle Gangs, because it is these groups that are actively involved in criminal activity.

Outlaw Motorcycle Gangs (OMG)

Adolafia
American Iron (SOS)
Amigos (BAN)
Ancient Iron
Avengers
Bacchus (HA)
Bandidos
Bandoleers
Barons
Barrio Riders
Bay Riders (HA)
Bishops (HA)
Black Pistons (OUT)
Black Widows (BAN)
Blatnois (HA)
Branded Ones
Broken Dreams
Brothers Speed (V)
Bull Shit (BAN)
Burning Skulls
Calavera (BAN)
Canpesinos (BAN)
Ching - A - Ling
Chosen Ones
Coffin Cheaters
Cumplidores (BAN)
Damners (HA)
Death Hands
Death Riders (HA)
Defiant Few (HA)
Defiant Souls (SOS)
Demon Keepers (HA)
Desgraciados (BAN)
Destralos (BAN)
Destroyer (HA)
Deuces Wild (SOS)
Devils Disciples
Devils Dolls
Diablos (SOS) (BAN)
Dirty Dozen
Disciples
El Forastero
Evil Ones (HA)
Exiles Motorcycle Club
Fandango Confederate
Freewheelers
Galloping Goose
Gringos
Gypsies (OUT)
Freedom Riders (HA)
Ghetto Riders
Ghost Mountain Riders
Ghost Riders
Grim Reapers (HA)
Guerrilleros (BAN)
Gypsy Jokers
Hell-bent
Hells Angels
Hell's Lovers (African American)
Hermanons (BAN)
Hessians
Highlanders (HA)
Highplains Drifters
Highwaymen
Hombres (BAN)
Huns
Iron Crossmen
Iron Horsemen (SOS)
Jackals (HA)
Kerberos (HA)
Killerbeez (BAN)
Kinsmen (HA)
L.A. Riders (BAN)
Legion of Doom
Lone Skull (OUT)
Loners
Lonesome Fugitives
Los Bravos (BAN)
Los Dorados (BAN)
Los Peros (BAN)
Mestizoz (BAN)
Malditos (BAN)
Misfits
Molochs
Mongols
Mountain Men (SOS)
New Blood
Novalis (BAN)
Odin's Warriors
OK Riders (BAN)
Outlaws
Pagans
Palmers (BAN)
Para-Dice Riders (HA)
Paisanos (BAN)
Peligrosos (BAN)
Pissed Off Bastards of Bloomington
Pistoleros (BAN)
Raiders (MON)
Rebels (HA)
Red Devils (HA)

Red Line Crew (HA)
Regulators (HA)
Renegades (BAN)
Rising Suns
Road Bros (BAN)
Road Rage (BAN)
Road Tramps
Roca (BAN)
Rock Hell City Crew
Rock Machine (BAN)
Rockers (HA)
Rowdy Crew (HA)
Salty Dogs (BAN)
Satan's Choice (HA)
Satan's Disciples
Satan's Guards (HA)
Sidewinders (HA)
Silent Few (SOS)
Silent Rebels (SOS)
Silent Sinners (SOS)
Sin City Disciples (African-American)
Skeleton Crew
Soldados (BAN)
Soldiers of Islam (BAN)
Solo Angles (Mexico)
Sons of Aesir
Sons of Darkness (African-American)
Sons of Hell (HA)
Sons of Silence
Southsiders (BAN)
Steel City Crew (BAN)
Spartan Riders (HA)
The Dirty Whites (HA)
The Foundation (HA)
The Grim Reapers
The King's Crew
The Malditos (HA)
The Men
Tophatters
Tribes
Thunderguards
Unforgiven (HA)
Vagabonds
Vagos
Valiants
Valhalla (HA)
Vaqueros (BAN)
Vikings
Villistas (BAN)
Wanted
Warlocks
Wrecking Machine (HA)
Wheels of Soul

Note:

African-American	=	Refers to clubs that are only made up of predominantly African-American members.
BAN	=	Reported affiliates of the Bandidos
HA	=	Reported affiliates of the Hells Angels
OUT	=	Reported affiliates of the Outlaws
MEX	=	Refers to OMGs located mainly in Mexico
MON	=	Reported affiliates of the Mongols
SOS	=	Reported affiliates of the Sons of Silence
V	=	Reported affiliates of the Vagos

Every motorcycle club or gang listed above is known to be an outlaw motorcycle club/gang or support for/affiliate with "outlaw motorcycle gangs (OMGs)" through their public support of OMGs, criminal activity, writings, publications, and/or postings.

Law Enforcement/Emergency Services/Veteran and Armed Forces Motorcycle Clubs

5-0 MC
A.C.E.
American Fire Fighters
American Lawman
American Knights
American Legion Riders
Angels of Fire
Archangels
Blood Brothers
Blue Iron
Blue Knights
Buffalo Soldiers
Caballero Aguila
Celtic Law
Centurions
Choir Boys
City Heat
Combat Vets
Copperheads
Delta Posse
Dragon Slayers
E.O.D.
Enforcers
Fine Riders
Fire Hogs
Gatekeepers
Grey Dragons
Guardians
Gunfighters
Guns and Fire
Hangmen
Hard Chargers
Iron Crew
Iron Knights
Iron Order
Iron Pigs
Iron Warriors
Law Enforcement Riders
Law Dawgs
Law Riders
Leathernecks
Legacy Vets
Lords of Loyalty
Los Carnales
Maltese Knights
Nam Knights
Paladins
Patriot Guard
Praetorian
Rescue Riders
Red Knights
Regulators
Renegade Pigs
Road Dawgs
Roll'n Thunder
Roughnecks
Sentinels
Smoking Guns
Swords of Justice
Special Forces MC
Streets of Fire
Thin Blue Line MC
Veterans MS
Veterans of Vietnam
VFW Warriors
Viet Nam Vets
Untouchables
Warthogs
Wild Pigs
Wind and Fire

Although each of the above named motorcycle clubs appear to be outlaw motorcycle gangs because of their style of dress, the majority of the members of these clubs are either active or retired law enforcement officers and/or Emergency Service/Veteran and Armed Forces workers. These groups are social clubs rather than gangs that are not involved in criminal activity. The purpose of including this information in this text is to enable the reader to distinguish between outlaw motorcycle gangs and Public Safety motorcycle clubs.

Motorcycle Gangs/Clubs Tattoo Symbols and Marks

Out of Club in Bad Standing

Out of Club in Good Standing

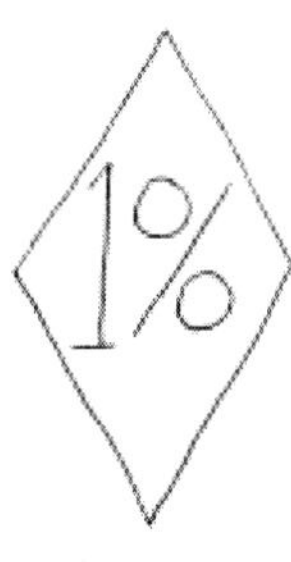

Outlaw Biker Club

Stands for the Letter M

Meth, Marijuana or Motorcycle

Motorcycle Club

Other Outlaw Motorcycle Gang Symbols and Acronyms Commonly Used in Tattooing, Writing, and Worn on Vests/Colors/Cuts

1%

Means that the wearer considers himself part of the 1% of motorcycle riders that take part in criminal activity and he is a member of an outlaw motorcycle gang.

13

Refers to the thirteenth letter of the alphabet "M." The "M" refers to either Marijuana or Meth. The wearer of this number may be a user or a dealer of either drug.

Charlie

The nickname of the Outlaws M.C. center patch.

BFFB

The first and last letters refer to the outlaw motorcycle gang in question. In this example Bandidos are the OMG in question. BFFB means "Bandidos Forever, Forever Bandidos." Almost every OMG will use this marking by substituting their group's name. Another example would be "Mongols forever, forever Mongols." This acronym is also used by non-OMG motorcycle clubs.

Death Head

The nickname of the Hells Angels M.C. center patch.

Domec Mors Non Separat

Even in death we will not separate (Inspection at the bottom of the SOS center patch.)

Fat Mexican

The nickname of the Bandidos M.C. center patch.

Feather Head

Center patch of the Hells Angels Colors.

M

Means Marijuana, Meth, or Motorcycle. The wearer of this letter maybe a user and or dealer of the aforementioned drugs. Sometimes the letter M is said to mean motorcycle.

Mammas
A woman that is the property of an OMG

MC
Stands for Motorcycle Club.

MG
Stands for Motorcycle Gang.

National (accompanied by office title)
Means the wearer holds a national office within the organization.

NTAA
Nomad Tested and Approved.

Old Lady
A woman who is married to a full patch member of an OMG.

OMG
Outlaw Motorcycle Gang.

Probate, Prospect, or Probationary
Means the wearer is a probationary member of a motorcycle gang or club. The color of the lettering will coincide with OMG's club colors. This term is used by both outlaw and non-outlaw motorcycle clubs.

President, Secretary, Sergeant at Arms, etc.
Means the wearer holds said office in a local chapter.

Run
A required trip taken on motorcycles by the gang or club that is generally carried out in formation.

Sheep
A woman that is the property of an OMG

Surtr
The nickname of the Pagan's M.C. center patch.

Sweeties
A woman who moves from full patch member to full patch member with in an OMG.

Reading Outlaw and Other Motorcycle Gang/Club Colors (Three Patch System)

Male Colors

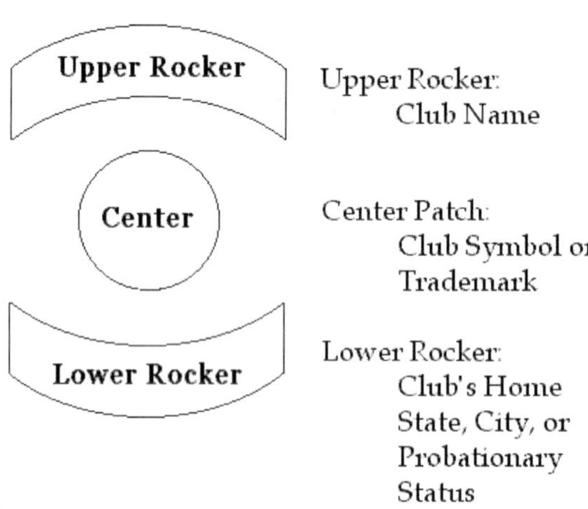

The now famous "Three Patch System" used by not only outlaw motorcycle gangs, but motorcycle clubs of all kinds, is normally displayed in one of the three following manners:

1. On a vest made out of any material (leather or denim).
2. On a jacket (leather or denim normally).
3. Tattooed on a person's back or body.

Note: The Pagans do not use a lower rocker that identifies them with an area or location and the SOS use only a center patch and bottom rocker.

Female Colors

Property

of

Club Name

or

Member's Name

It is not uncommon to see colors in the above fashion displayed by female "members" of Outlaw Motorcycle Gangs. The actual color of the patches will be the same as their male counterparts. The rules of the Outlaw Motorcycle Gang will determine if the bottom patch states the name of the gang or the name of the woman's boyfriend or husband in the gang. Some female "members" will also display a unique center patch similar to their male counterparts.

General Outlaw Motorcycle Gang History

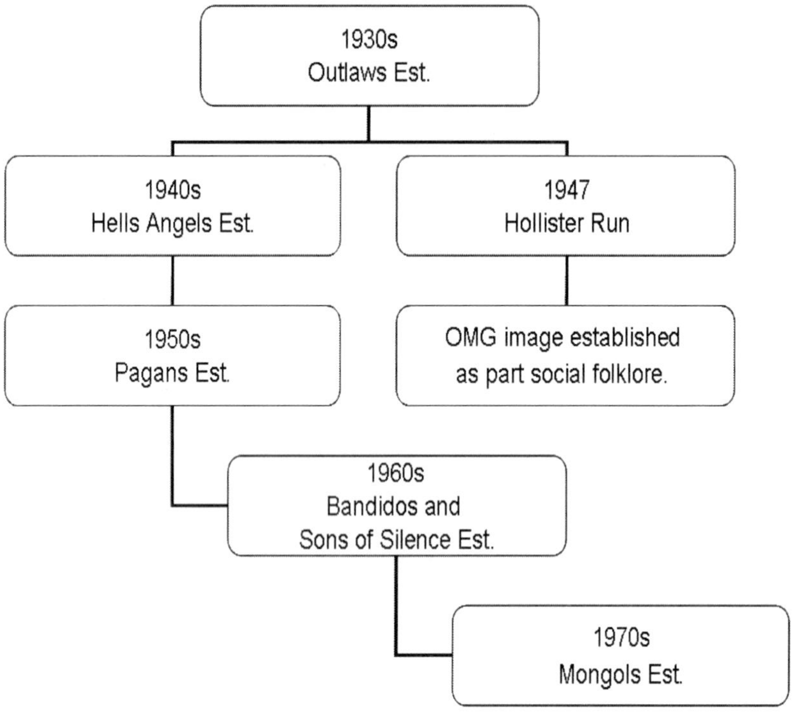

The first highly publicized criminal activity involving outlaw motorcycle gangs took place in Hollister, California in 1947. Although many of the accounts of the activities that took place in Hollister were exaggerated and, in some cases, outright lies, the image of the outlaw motorcycle gang member was captured in a staged photograph published in *Life* magazine. The OMG's image became a part of the social folklore and a common vision in the minds of many Americans due to the media coverage that followed the Hollister incident.

Following the Hollister incident, the original chapters of the Hell's Angels motorcycle club made their now famous Porterville "run" in 1963, which firmly secured the outlaw motorcycle gang in American culture. The lifestyle of the outlaw motorcycle gangs and their members became more public throughout the 1950s and 1960s thanks to Hollywood and other media outlets that often trade truth for action-packed fallacies. The lifestyle of the outlaw biker that was portrayed for the American public was almost romantic to those that didn't know the truth about how violent OMGs are. This romantic portrayal created "the freedom of the open road and living by one's own rules" myth that so many weekend warriors strive to attain and has led to the mimicking of OMG dress by so many riding clubs.

Specific Histories of the "Big Six" and Other OMGs

1. HELLS ANGELS MOTORCYCLE CLUB

Type of Gang: Non-traditional

Founded: Late 1940s

Founded by: Members of the Pissed Off Bastards of Bloomington in San Bernardino, California

General racial makeup: Caucasian and Hispanic

Main rivals: All other motorcycle gangs

Headquarters: Oakland, California

Chapters:
250 plus chapters in the United States of America.
Chapters in twenty-nine plus countries outside of the U.S.A.
Over 193 chapters world wide.

Estimated number of members: 2,500 plus

Major historical events:
1946—future members involved in the Hollister violence.
1957—the third chapter of the Hells Angels is created in Oakland California.
Late 1950s—Ralph H. "Sonny" Barger is elected president of the Oakland Chapter.

Late 1950s until present—Sonny Barger turns the Hells Angels into a criminal enterprise.
1963—the original chapters of the Hells Angels motorcycle club made their now famous Porterville "run."
1966—The Hells Angels become a corporation.
2002—Hells Angels' members and Mongol members are involved in a shootout in the Harrah's Casino in Laughlin, Nevada.
2002—a HA shoot-on-site order is given for all Mongol members.
1950 until present—the Hells Angels are targeted by law enforcement.

2. The Bandidos Motorcycle Club

Type of Gang: Non-traditional

Founded: 1966

Founded by: Motorcycle club members from Houston or San Leon, Texas

General racial makeup: Caucasian and Hispanic.

Main rivals: All other outlaw motorcycle gangs

Headquarters: Corpus Christi Texas

Chapters:
30 plus chapters in the United States
Chapters in fourteen plus countries outside of the U.S.A.

Estimated number of members: 500 plus

Main historical events:
1966 to present—the Bandidos have been targeted by law enforcement.
2011—New "updated" patch introduced in the United States.

3. THE OUTLAWS MOTORCYCLE CLUB

Type of Gang: Non-traditional

Founded: 1930s

Founded by: Member of the McCook Outlaws in McCook, Illinois

General racial makeup: Caucasian and Hispanic

Main rivals: All other outlaw motorcycle gangs

Headquarters: Detroit, Michigan

Chapters:
34 plus chapters in the United States of America
Chapters in four plus countries outside of the U.S.A.

Estimated number of members: 900 plus

Major historical events:
1947—declared war on the Hells Angels.
1950s—moved into Chicago and began calling themselves the Outlaw Nation.
1950s until present—the Outlaw Nation has been targeted by law enforcement.
1965-66—became known as the Outlaw Nation.
2010—Twenty-seven members of the American Outlaw Association (Outlaws MC) are indicted by authorities.

4. MONGOLS MOTORCYCLE CLUB

Type of Gang: Non-traditional

Founded: Early 1970s

Founded by: Motorcycle club members in the Los Angeles area

General racial makeup: Caucasian and Hispanic

Main rivals: All other outlaw motorcycle gangs

Headquarters: San Gabriel Valley, California

Chapters:
19 plus nationwide chapters
Chapters in three plus countries outside of the U.S.A.

Estimated number of members: 500 plus

Major historical events:
1970s to present—the Mongols have been targeted by law enforcement.
Late 1990s—the Bureau of Alcohol, Tobacco and Firearms (BATF) declared the Mongols "The most dangerous outlaw gang in the country."
2000—a three-year undercover investigation by BATF Special Agent William Queen ends.
2002—the Mongols and the Hells Angels are involved in a shootout in the Harrah's Casino in Laughlin, Nevada.
2002—a shoot-on-site order is given for all Hells Angels members.
2008—undercover investigation by four BATF agents ends and the Mongol's trademark for their "colors" is suspended by the Federal Courts. Law enforcement officers are authorized to confiscate Mongol "colors" on sight for the first time in history. The Mongols begin wearing a new center patch.
2010—the Mongols begin wearing their original center patch again after lengthy legal battle.

5. Sons of Silence Motorcycle Club

Type of Gang: Non-traditional

Founded: 1966

Founded by: Bruce Richardson in Niwot and Denver, Colorado area

General racial makeup: Caucasian

Main rivals: All other outlaw motorcycle gangs

Headquarters: Colorado Springs, Colorado

Chapters:
30 plus nationwide chapters
Chapters in two plus countries outside of the U.S.A.

Estimated number of members: 325 plus

Major historical events:
Established a national chapter in 1968.
Late 1990s and early 2000s—began recruiting heavily.
1990s—undercover investigation carried out by the Bureau of Alcohol Tobacco and Firearms ends.
1990s to present—the SOS struggles to establish itself securely among the Big Six.

6. Pagans Motorcycle Club

Type of Gang: Non-traditional

Founded: Late 1950s in Maryland

Founded by: Lou Dobkins or Fred "Dutch" Buren

General Racial Makeup: Caucasian

Main rivals: All other outlaw motorcycle gangs

Headquarters: Long Island New York (location of chapters changes regularly)

Chapters:
44 plus chapters in the United States of America
Chapters in one plus countries outside of the U.S.A.

Estimated number of members: 900 plus

Major historical events:

2002—Attacked the Hells Angels in Long Island at the Hells Raisers Ball.

2005—Forced the Hells Angels to close Long Island chapter after the murder of the Hells Angel Long Island chapter president.

Comparatively there is less information known about the Pagans than the other members of the Big Six. The Pagans share the same criminal nature and power structure of other OMGs; however, their chapters are not nearly as stable as those of other OMGs. Currently the Pagans are headquartered in Pennsylvania.

7. The Warlocks Motorcycle Club

Type of Gang: Non-traditional

Founded: 1967

Founded by: Former members of the United States Navy, Orlando, Florida

General racial makeup: Caucasian and Hispanic

Main rivals: The Outlaws

Major historical events:

1991—Raymond Chaffin, president of the Warlocks is murdered in his garage in Edgewater, Florida.

July 2003—BATF undercover investigation ends in indictments and the arrest of 81 members and the largest single Outlaw Motorcycle Gang "take down" in BATF history.

8. The Vagos Motorcycle Club aka Green Nation

Type of Gang: Non-traditional

Founded: 1965

Founded by: Motorcycle gang members San Bernardino, California

General racial makeup: Caucasian and Hispanic

Main rivals: Other Motorcycle Clubs

Major historical events:

2000—Members are indicted on a variety of charges.

March 2006—BATF undercover investigation ends in indictments and the arrest of twenty plus members and is one of the largest single joint multi-jurisdictional operation to date.

Note: The first six Outlaw Motorcycle Gangs listed above are known as the "Big Six" (Hells Angels, Bandidos, Mongols, Sons of Silence, Outlaws, and the Pagans).

General Outlaw Motorcycle Gang Hierarchies

Outlaw Motorcycle Gang (National)

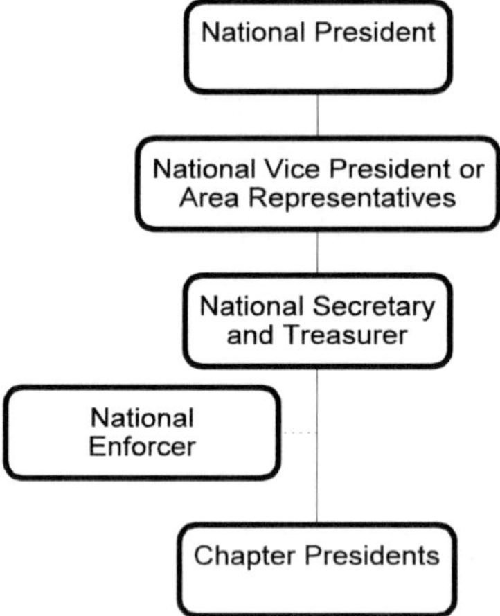

Outlaw Motorcycle Gang (State)

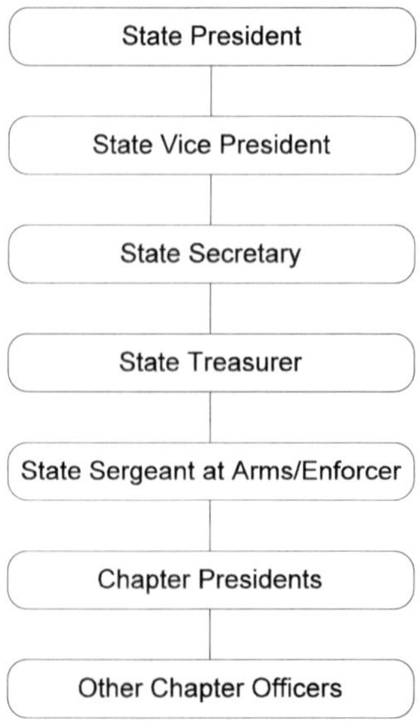

Outlaw Motorcycle Gang (Local)

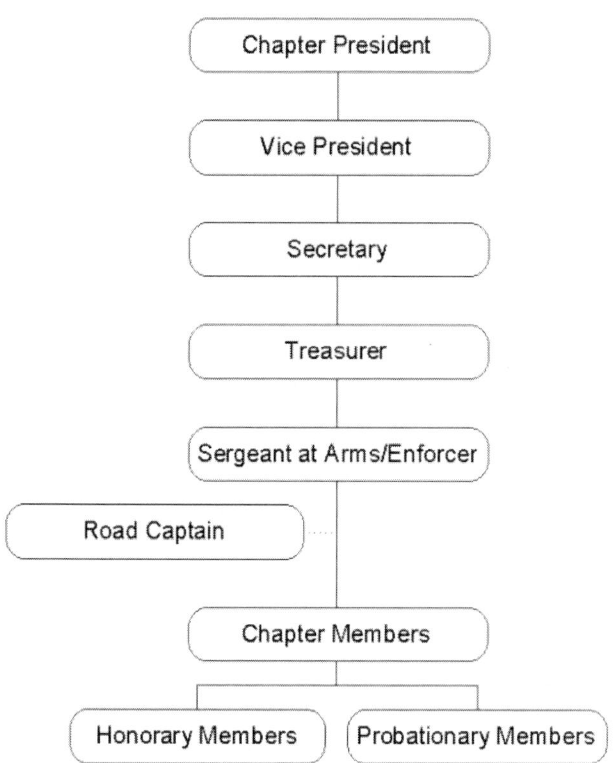

Note: Associates and hang rounds are not included in this hierarchy because they are not considered members of the gang; however, their level of influence in the group falls in the same arena as that of the honorary and probationary member.

Outlaw Motorcycle Gang (Nomad)

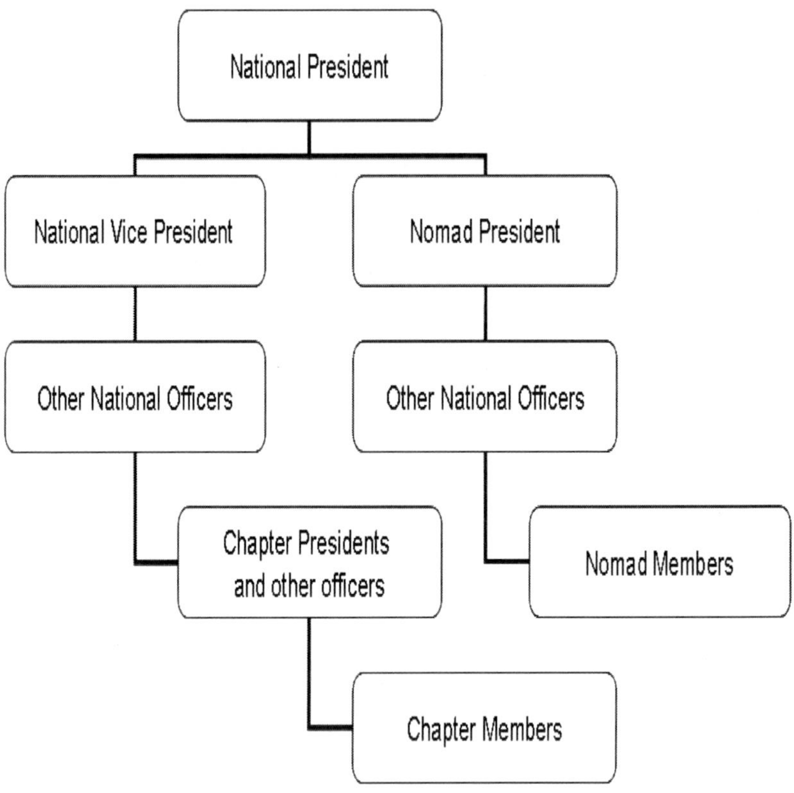

Note: Nomad OMGs do not claim a specific territory or area like local or national clubs do. Nomad club members often act as "reinforcements" for local clubs when additional members or members unrecognizable by other OMGs are needed.

Outlaw Motorcycle Gang Riding Formations

(FRONT)

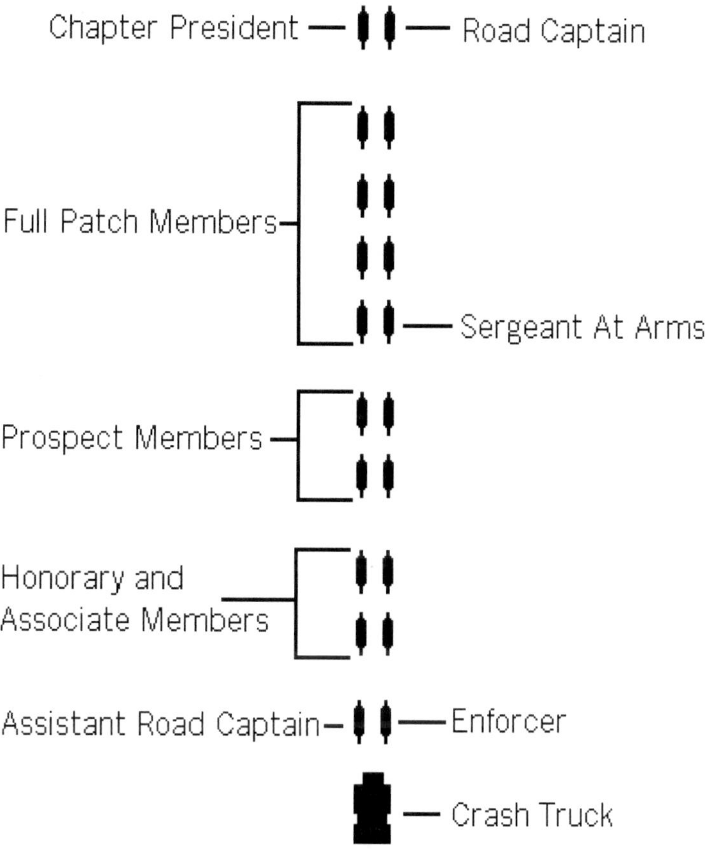

This is a typical formation used by Outlaw Motorcycle Gangs for group rides, although not all parts of this formation are present during every group ride. For instance, there may not always be honorary and associate members present during group rides. Furthermore, the crash truck often follows the formation from a distance and may not be easily recognizable. When attempting to identify the crash truck look for support stickers on the vehicle. The crash truck may be driven by a man or a woman and may contain weapons, narcotics, and other contraband.

OMG Recruitment

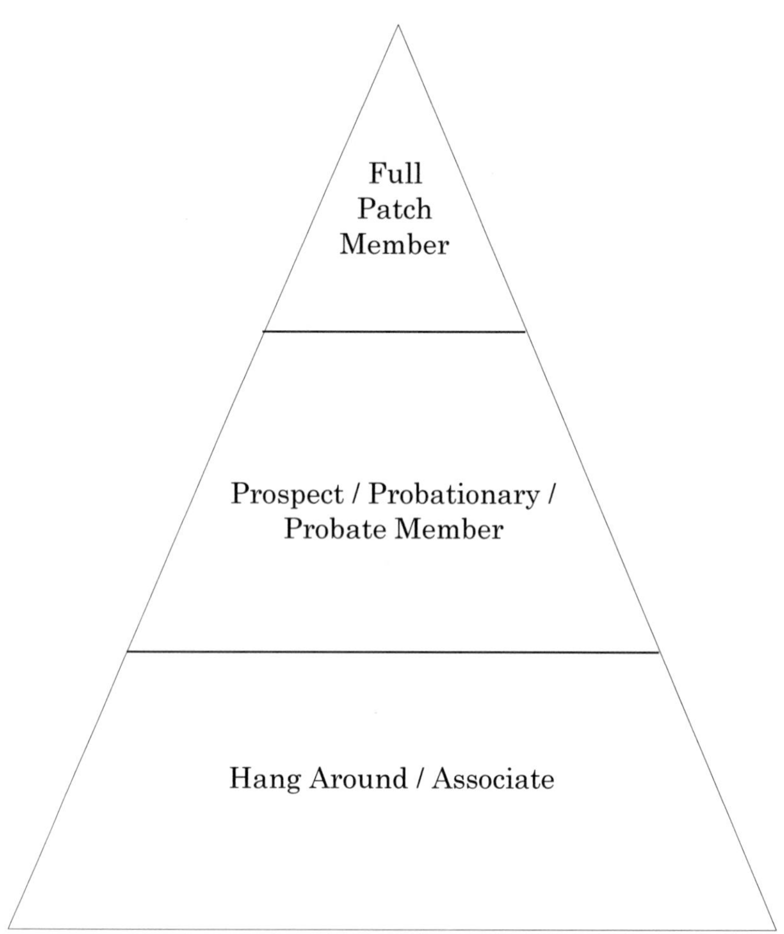

Introduction

The Folk and People Nation are based in Illinois and are a gang conglomeration in the same way that Sureño 13 and Norteño 14 are in California. Each Nation, be it either the People or Folk are made up of many subsets with diverse ethnic and cultural backgrounds. Sets in each Nation are just as likely to get along with each other as they are not. The main thing that holds each Nation together are the symbols that are universally used by the members of each Nation (i.e., the six-pointed star and pitchforks [Folk] or the five-pointed star and top hat [People]) and their hate of their rival nation.

Currently, the Folk Nation is controlled by the Gangster Disciples, which is headed by Larry Hoover who is currently serving multiple life sentences in the Federal Bureau of Prison in Florence, Colorado. The People Nation is currently led by the Latin Kings, but is not controlled by them in the same manner that the Gangster Disciples control the Folk Nation. The Gangster Disciples maintain much tighter control over Folk Nation sets then the Latin Kings have over People Nation sets. This example is easily illustrated in the Gangster Disciples ability to effectively tax the drug trade and manage members that are out of state and the Latin Kings inability to.

It is also common to find traditional West Coast gangs claiming affiliation with the Folk or People Nation in areas that are controlled by one of or both of the Nations; for example, Crips claim Folk Nation and Bloods claim People Nation in the Illinois area. Although these associations occurred as the result of the murder of "King David" (Folk) by a Blood, it is still an accurate example of the above fact. It is worth noting that these affiliations also fan the flames of the East Coast / West Coast rivals between traditionally West Coast gangs because West Coast Crips and Bloods feel that it is disrespectful to show respect to individuals (Larry Hoover) and groups (Folk and People Nation) that did not have anything to do with the founding of these gangs.

Note: In the Midwest and on the West Coast the Gangster Disciples are often referred to incorrectly as the Black Gangster Disciples. The gang led by Larry Hoover is the Gangster Disciples. The Black Disciples and the Black Gangsters are gangs with in the Folk Nation.

Folk Nation Affiliated Gangs

Allport Lovers
Almighty Harrison Gents
Ambrose
Asian Outcasts
Ashland Vikings
Black Souls
Black Disciples
Black Gangsters
Black Gangster Disciples
Brazers
Brother of the Struggle
Campbell Boys
City Knights
C-Note
Crip Nation
Cullerton Deuces
Florida Boys
Gangster Disciples
Gangster Party Boys
Ghetto Boys
Guess Boys
Harrison Gents
Imperial Gangsters
Imperial Spanish Gangsters
Insane Ashland Vikings
Insane Deuces
Insane Gangster Disciple
Insane Popes (North Side)
Insane Spanish Chancellors
Island Bound Sureno (Florida)
International Posse
Krazy Getdown Boys
La Raza
Latin Disciples
Latin Dragons (North Side)
Latin Eagles
Latin Jivers
Latin Lovers
Latin Souls
Latin Stylers
Maniac Latin Disciples
Memphis Boys
Milwaukee Kings
Morgan Boys
Murder Mobb
New Breed Black Gangsters
Orchestra Albany
Party People
Pump Nation
Racine Boys
Ridgeway Lords
Satan Disciples
Simon City Royals
Sister of the Struggle
Somali Gangster Disciples
Spanish Cobras
Spanish Gangster Disciples
Two One
Two Seven
Two Six Boys
Two Six Nation
Two Sixers
Two Two Boys
United Gangster Disciples
Young Gangster Disciples
Young Guns

People Nation Affiliated Gangs

12th Street Players
23rd Street Kings
Almighty Taylor Jousters
Bishops
Black P-Stone Nation
Black P-Stone
Black P-Stone Rangers
Blood Nation
Boulevard Latin King Nation
Bout Havin Money CVL Boys
Brown Pride Locos (Florida)
Central Insane VL
Chi West
Cicero Mafia Insane VL
Cobra Stones
Conservative Vice Lords (CVL)
CVL Boys
Cullerton Deuces
Eight Ball Posse
El Rukns
Executioners
Familia Stones
Five Star Elite TVL
Five Star Elite UVL
Four Corner Hustlers
Future Stones
Gaylords
Imperial Insane VL
Insane Popes (South Side)
Insane Unknowns
Insane VL
Junior Kings
Kenmore Boys
Kents
Killbourn Park Gaylord's
Latin Brothers
Latin Counts
Latin Dragons (South Side)
Latin Kings
Latin Mafia
Latin Pachucos
Latin Queens
Latin Saints
Latin Angels
Latin Stones
Loco Boys
Mafia VL
Mellow People
Metros
Mickey Cobras
Noble Knights
Pachucos
Palmer Street Gaylords
Park Avenue Players
Party Gents
PR Stones
Puerto Rican Players
Renegade VL
Spanish Lords
Spanish VL
Stone Kents
Stoned Freaks
Tiny Man Crew
Traveling Vice Lords (TVL)
Undertakers VL
Unknown Vice Lords (UL)
Universidad Vice Lords (UVL)
Vice Lords (VL)
Villalobos
War Lords
Wild Walker Kings
Young Money Getta's

Vice Lord Nation

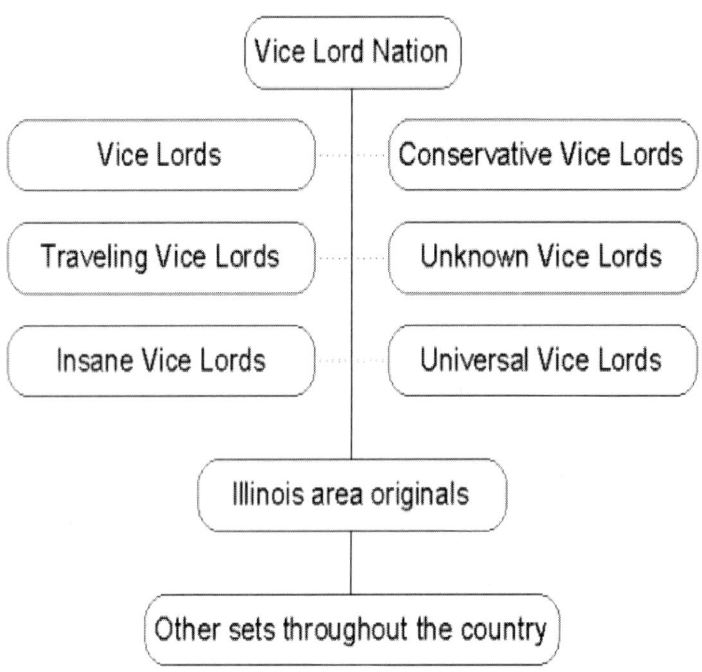

Folk Nation Tattoo, Symbols, Graffiti, and Marks

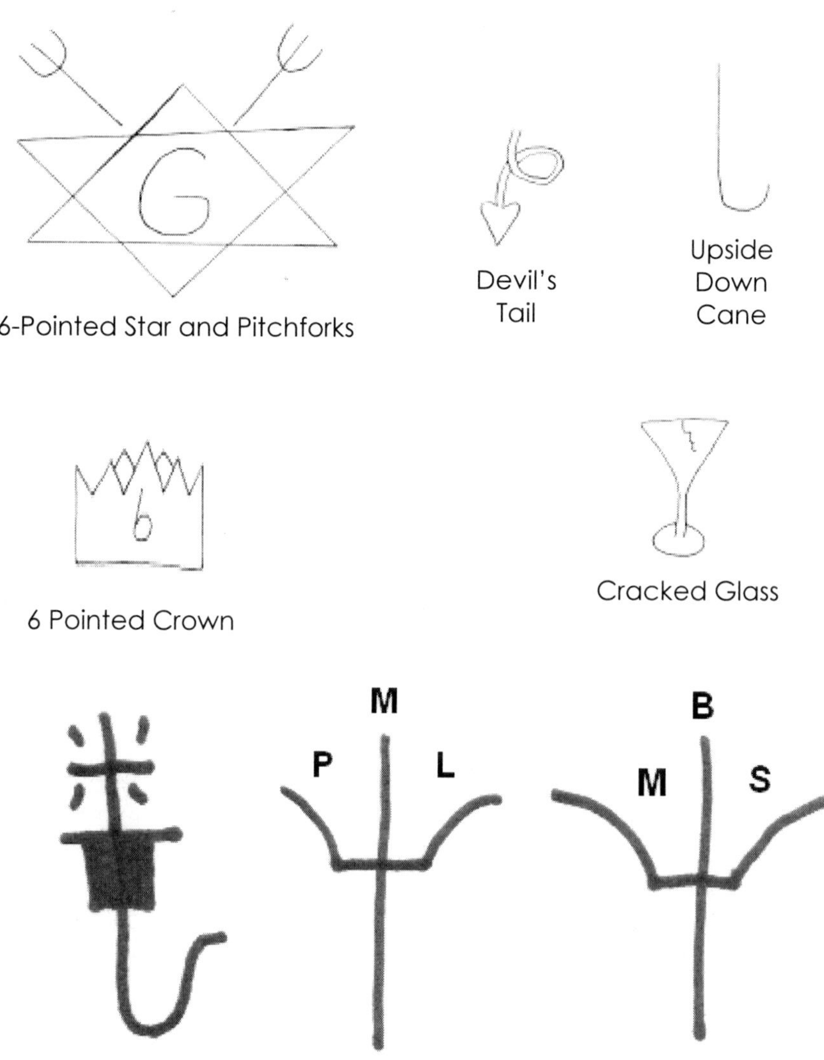

6-Pointed Star and Pitchforks

Devil's Tail

Upside Down Cane

6 Pointed Crown

Cracked Glass

Hook and Hat

Plenty Much Love

Mind Body Soul

Third World Disciple Nation

Disciple Love

The Love and Growth of the Folk Nation

Six-Pointed Star of the Folk Nation and the Meaning of Each Point

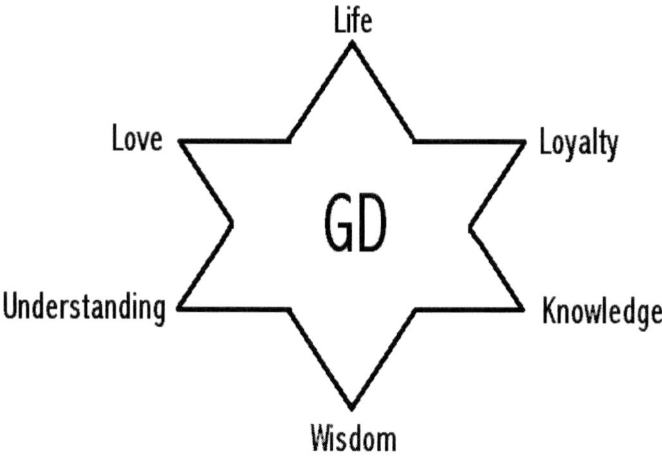

Note: Members of the Folk Nation and the Gangster Disciples dress and show respect and power to the right and to the right side of their bodies.

Other Common Folk Nation Abbreviations and Symbols Used in Tattooing and Graffiti

2-15-9	=	B.O.S. or Brothers of the Struggle
3.W.D.N	=	Third World Disciple Nation
6-15-12-11	=	Folk
19-15-19	=	S.O.S. or Sisters of the Struggle
24	=	B.D. or Black Disciples
74	=	Gangster Disciples
360	=	Knowledge, number of bricks on the yellow brick road of knowledge
720	=	Instruction of knowledge, number of bricks when you return on the yellow brick road of knowledge.
A.B.T.M.T.	=	All Bout That Money Thang
ADIDAS	=	All Day I Dream About Sheba or All Day Insane Disciple Against Slobs
B.D.	=	Black Disciple
B.G.D.	=	Better Growth and Development or Black Gangster Disciples
B.G.D.N.	=	Black Gangster Disciples Nation
B.O.S.(S)	=	Brothers of the Struggle (Street Struggle)
FOLKS	=	1. Following Our Loving King Shorty 2. Follow Obey (all) Laws (the) Kings Set 3. Followers (of) Our Last King Steps 4. Followers (of) Our Last King
G.D.	=	Gangster Disciples or Growth and Development
G.D.N.	=	Gangster Disciples Nation
Heart	=	The Love of the Nation (see above illustration)
I.G.D.	=	Insane Gangster Disciple
KSWISS	=	Kill Slob When I See Slob
L.L.L.	=	Life, Love, Loyalty
M.B.S.	=	Mind, Body, Soul (see above illustration)
M.G.D.	=	Manic Gangster Disciples
M.M.M.	=	Money, Mac, Murder
Pitch Forks	=	Peace and War (see above illustration)
P.M.L.	=	Plenty Much Love (see above illustration)
REEBOK	=	Read Each & Every Book of Knowledge
S.O.S.	=	Sisters of the Struggle
Tail	=	All things must come to an end

V.L.K.	=	Vice Lord Killer
Wings	=	Growth and Development of the Nation (see above illustration)
W.K.U.	=	Wisdom, Knowledge, Understanding

Note: The F.O.L.K.S. version of FOLK uses the "S" to represent the word Shorty. "King Shorty" is one of the Black Gangster Disciples Kings. However, this version is not often used because it shows respect to someone other then Larry Hoover, the acknowledged leader of the Folk Nation.

People Nation Tattoo, Symbols, Graffiti, and Marks

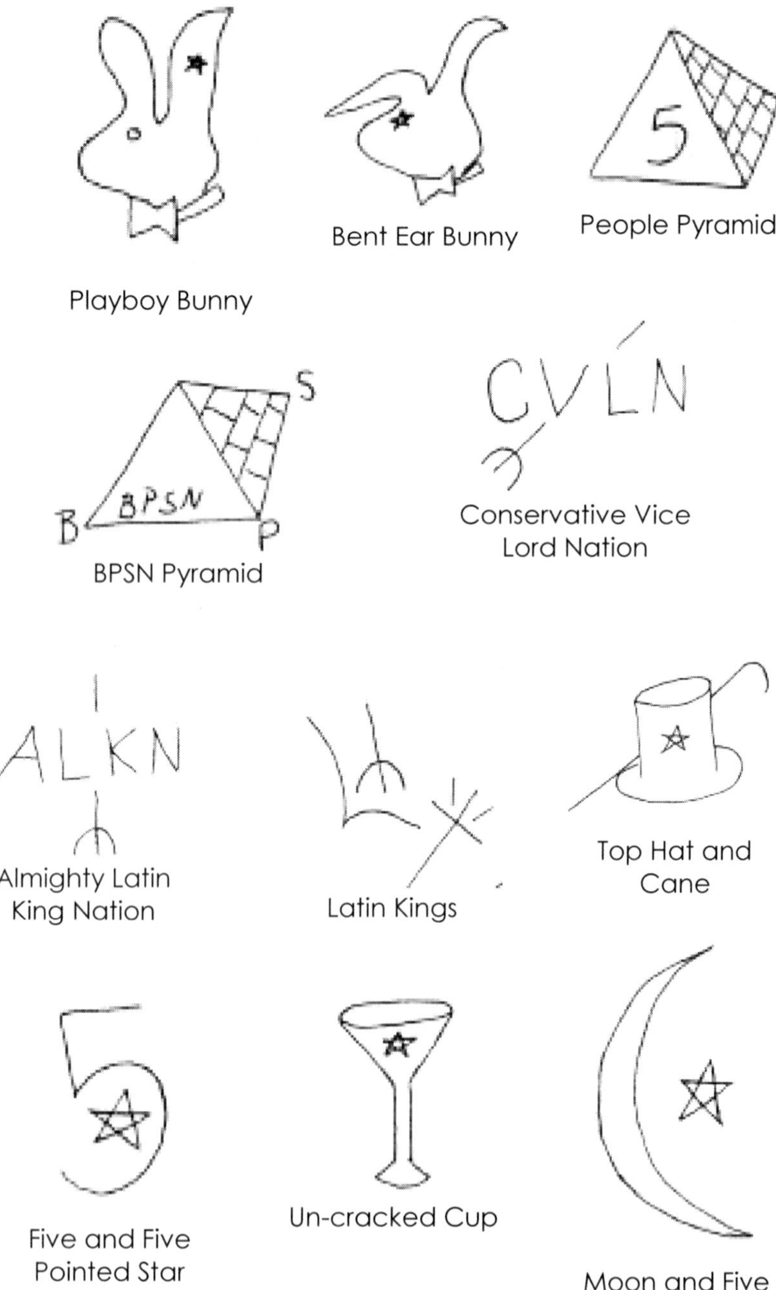

Playboy Bunny

Bent Ear Bunny

People Pyramid

BPSN Pyramid

Conservative Vice Lord Nation

Almighty Latin King Nation

Latin Kings

Top Hat and Cane

Five and Five Pointed Star

Un-cracked Cup

Moon and Five Pointed Star

Five-Pointed Star of the People Nation and the Meaning of Each Point

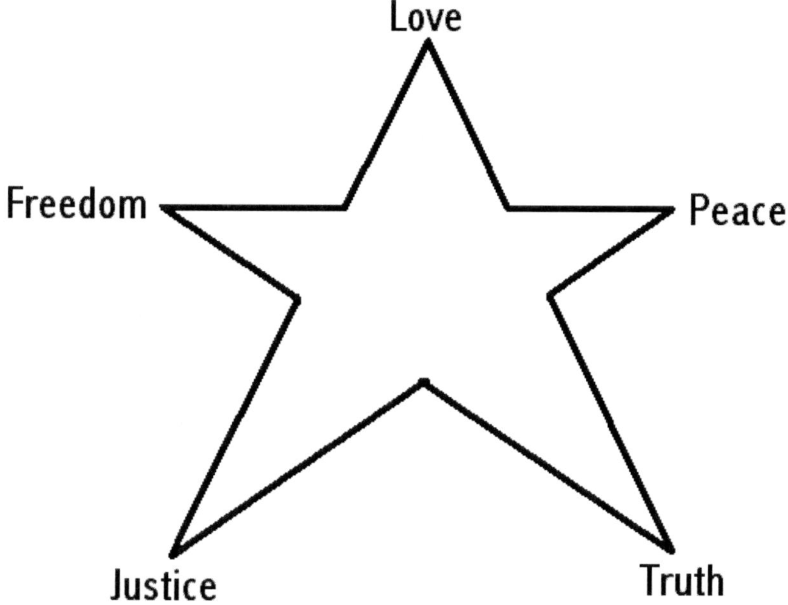

Note: Members of the People Nation and the Latin Kings dress and show respect and power to the left and to the left side of their bodies.

History of Black Gangster Disciples (Folk Nation)

Black Gangster Disciples a.k.a. Gangster Disciple Nation
BGD

Type of Gang: Traditional

Founded: Early 1960s

Founded by: Larry Hoover, David Barksdale, and Jerome Freeman

General ethnic makeup: African-American

Main rivals: People Nation gangs

Key historical event:

Was formed when Black Disciples (Devils) or the Supreme Gangster Nation, Black King Cobras, and Gangster Disciples unified.

Led by David Barksdale until 1972 when he was shot by a Blood named Adam Ford.

Early 1970s—Larry Hoover is sentenced to 150–200 years for ordering a murder.

The Black Gangster Disciples split into two groups in 1974: the Gangster Disciples led by Larry Hoover and the Black Disciples led by George Davis.

1980s—Gangster Disciples and Black Disciples battle for turf.

Larry Hoover forms Growth and Development, a grassroots political movement with Wallace "Gator" Bradley.

Helped form the Folk Nation between 1970 and 1980 in the Illinois state correctional system.

August 31, 1995—Larry Hoover is convicted of taxing (10%) the narcotics sales of Chicago gangs and is sent to Federal Prison under R.I.C.O.

History of the Chicago Latin Kings (People Nation)

THE ALMIGHTY LATIN KING AND QUEEN NATION (PEOPLE NATION)
"LKQN"

Type of Gang: Traditional

Founded: 1941 as the Young Lords

Founded by: Papa King Santos (originally a member of The Young Lords in New York) (deceased), Fast Eddy, Joe Rivera (Cadillac Joe), Eddie Rodriguez (Tiger) and Joe Gunn.

General ethnic makeup: Puerto Rican and Hispanic

Main rivals: Folk Nation gangs

Major historical events:

1959—became known as the Royal Kings.

Between 1964 and 1965—became known as the Latin Kings.

The original founding members Papa King Santos, Fast Eddy, Joe Rivera "Cadillac Joe," Eddy Rodriguez "Tiger," and Joe Gunn, become known as the "King of Kings."

1967—LKQN becomes a corporation in Chicago.

1970s and 1980s—the LKQN moved into Connecticut and New York.

Groups outside of Chicago become known as the "Bloodline" and "Tribes."

1990s to early 2000—King Tone attempts to change the New York LKQN into a political movement but fails after he is sent to prison.

Helped form the People Nation between 1970 and 1980 in the Illinois state correctional system.

Chicago and New York Nations, excluding the Bloodline, merge in 2007 or 2008.

Other People Nation Gang Histories

VICE LORDS (PEOPLE NATION)

Type of Gang:	Traditional
Founded:	Late 1950s within the juvenile correctional system in Illinois
Founded by:	Edward Perry
General ethnic makeup:	African American
Main Rivals:	Folk Nation gang and Gangster Disciples.

Major historical events:

Became known as the Vice Lord Nation.
Conservative Vice Lords (CVL) were created in 1964 as a subset of the Vice Lord Nation.
1960s—CVL became a corporation with the goal of helping their community.
In the early 1970s the CVL receives federal funding. Leader Bobby Gore is sent to prison for murder.
In the early 1980s the CVL returns to its criminal roots after collapse within the leadership.

BLACK P-STONE RANGERS (PEOPLE NATION)

Type of Gang:	Traditional
Founded:	Early 1960s
Founded by:	Jeff Fort and Eugene Hairston
General ethnic makeup:	African American
Main rivals:	Folk Nation gangs

Major historical events:

Originally called the Black Stone Rangers.
Created a governing body called the "Main 21."
Formed an alliance called the P-Stone Nation.
First gang to receive federal funds (thousands of dollars in "anti-poverty funding").
Jeff Fort is sent to federal prison in 1972.
Upon Fort's release from prison he creates a group called the El Rukns from members of the P-Stone Nation.
In the 1980s the El Rukns attempt to buy a rocket launcher in order to carry out terrorist for-hire activities for the Libyans.
Helped form the People Nation between 1970 and 1980 in the Illinois state correctional system.

FOUR CORNER HUSTLERS (PEOPLE NATION)

Type of Gang: Traditional

Founded: Early 1970s

Founded by: Walter Wheat

General racial makeup: African American

Major rivals: Folk Nation gangs and the Vice Lords

Major historical events:

In the early 1990s plotted to blow up a Chicago Police Station.
Numerous leadership changes in the 1990s due to infighting and murders.
Currently one of Chicago's largest street gangs.

Folk and People Nation General Migration from Illinois

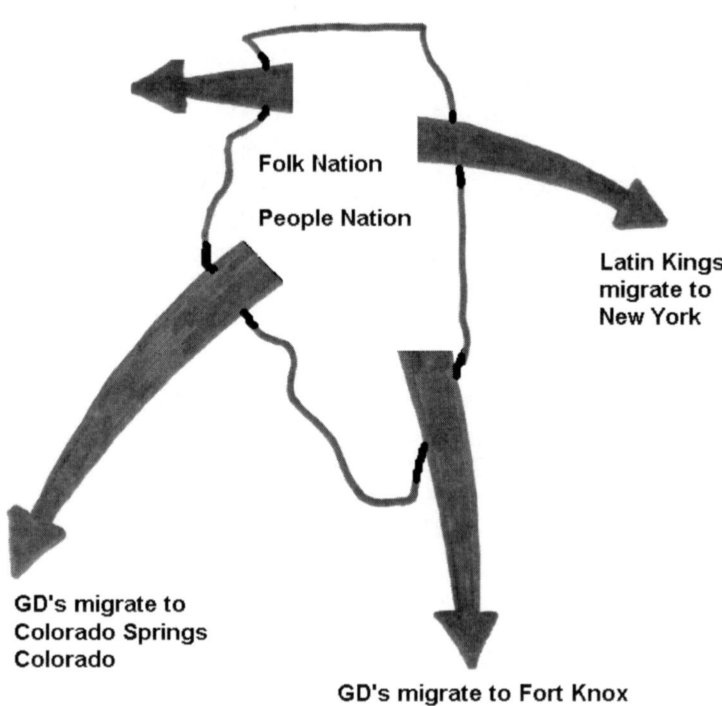

Although the GDs and the Latin Kings are two of the biggest street gangs to migrate from Illinois, many others have followed including the Vice Lords. All of these gangs, as well as many others, have migrated throughout the United States and into surrounding countries.

Chicago Latin Kings Migration

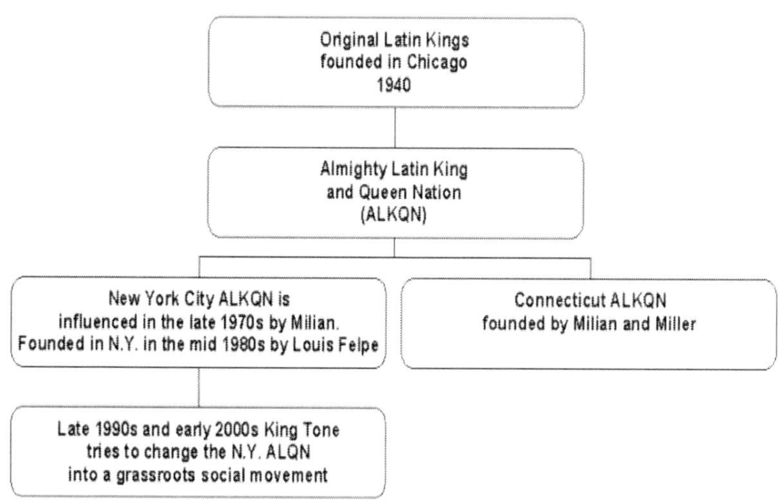

Millet and Millian are both members of the Almighty Latin King and Queen Nation who were incarcerated in prisons outside of Illinois. There are differing opinions as to the full names of Millet and Millian. Almighty Latin King and Queen Nation branches outside of Chicago are commonly referred to as tribes and as the Bloodline.

Gangster Disciples Hierarchy

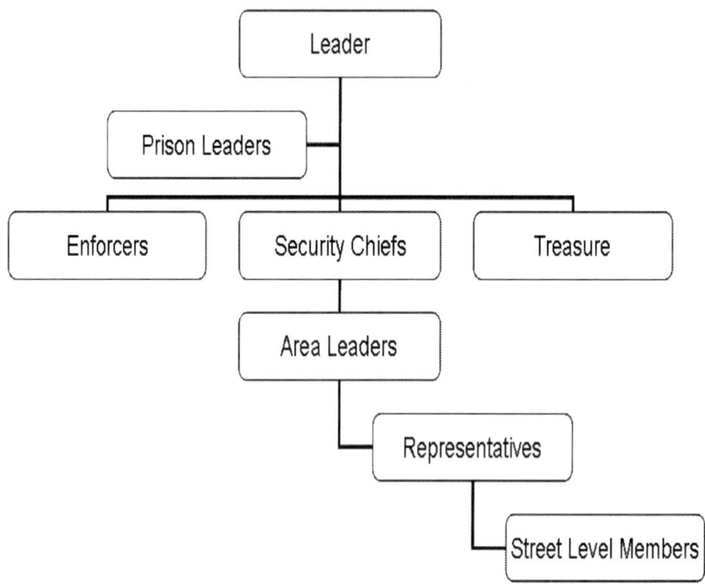

Latin King Hierarchy (Street and Correctional Facility)

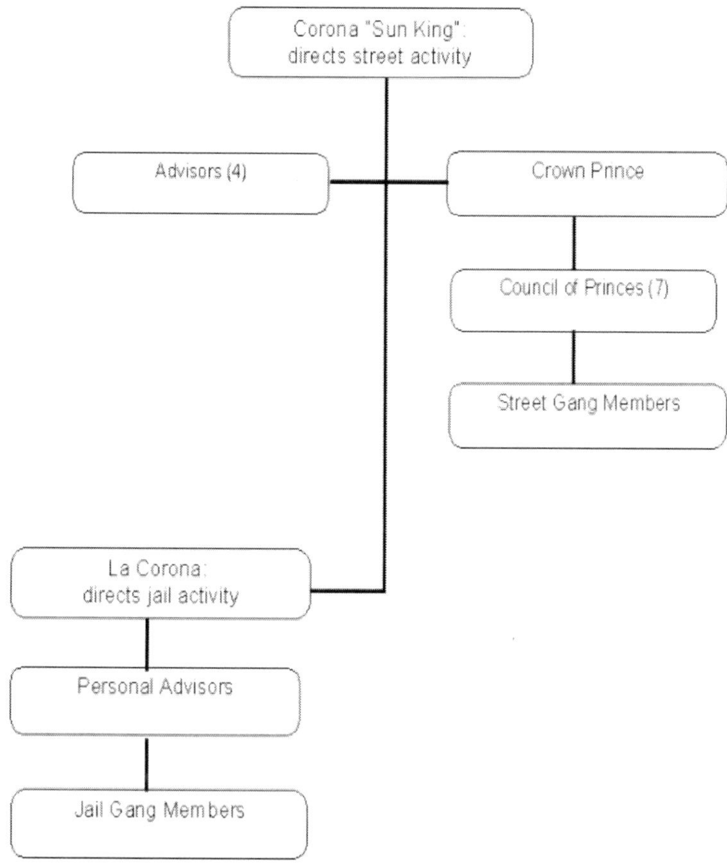

Council of Princes is made up of the heads of each arm of the gang and implements the goals set by the Corona and La Corona.

Latin King Hierarchy (Correctional Facilities)

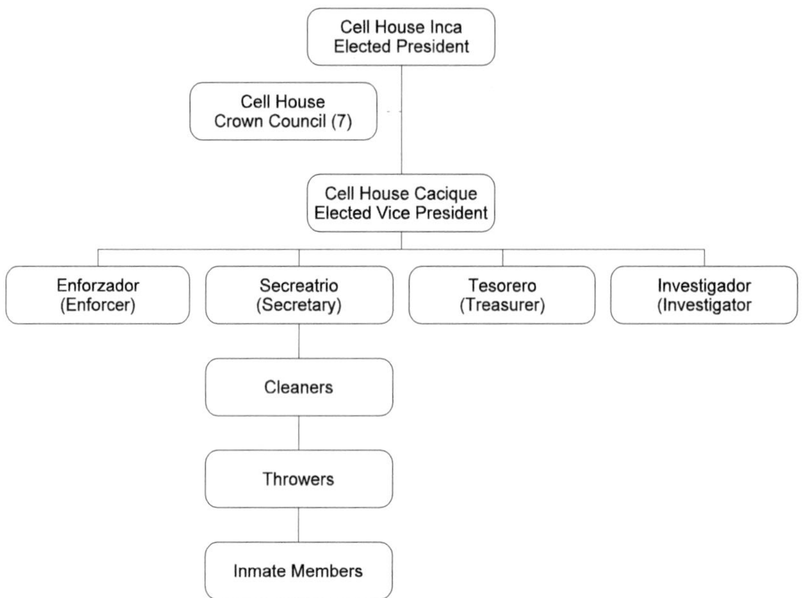

Latin King Hierarchy (Street Sub Leadership)

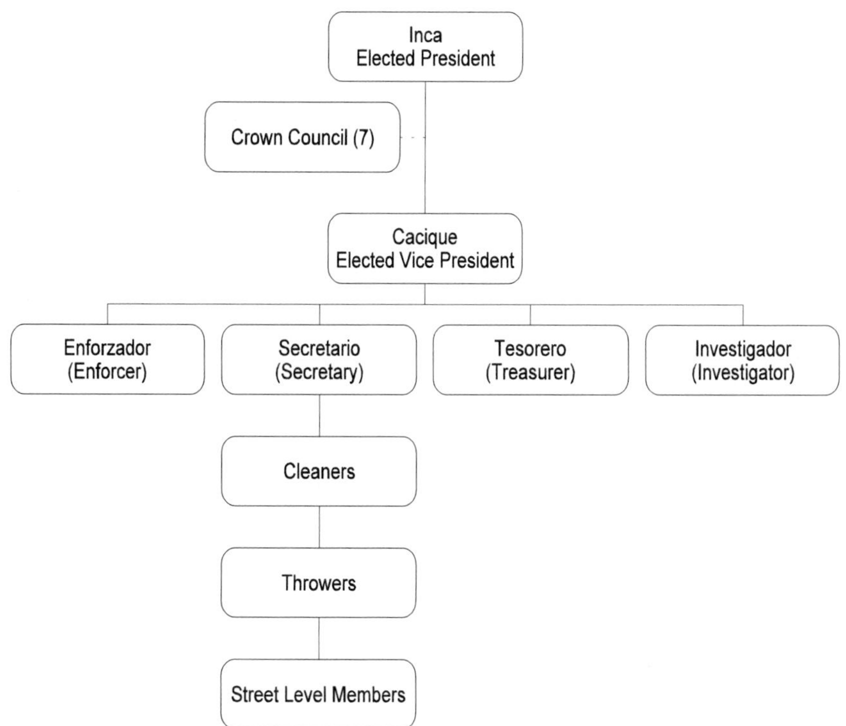

Colorado Latin King Tribes (2011)

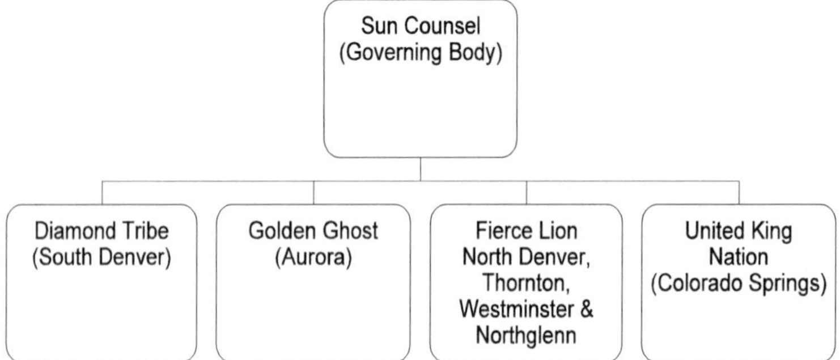

Colorado Latin Kings Hierarchy (2011)

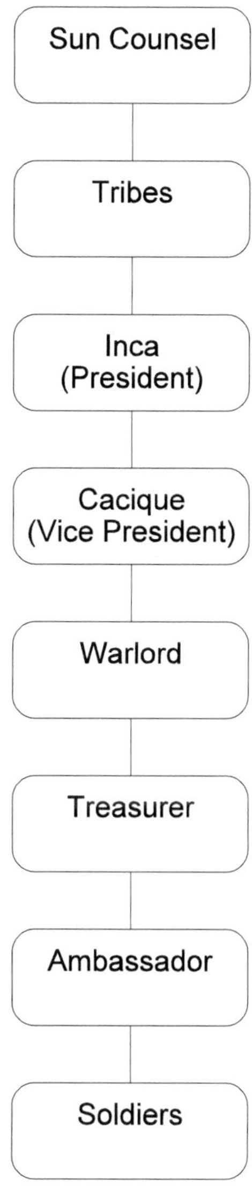

Introduction

Classically, criminal White Supremacist Groups and White Supremacy Groups are viewed as a group of poorly educated, hateful, misguided Caucasians of European decent with little better to do than to make a spectacle of themselves and stockpile weapons for a Race War that has yet to come; however, the truth is, these groups are made up of people from all walks of life including diverse social and economic backgrounds. Many of the people that hold supremacy beliefs look and act like everyday citizens while in public even though they harbor a variety of racial and/or ethnic based hatreds for those around them.

It is also important to understand that many of these so-called White Supremacy Groups and gangs accept members of diverse and mixed racial and ethnic backgrounds as long as the prospective member is not of African-American or Jewish decent. With this said, there are still exceptions. An example of this aforementioned fact is that one of the most powerful men in the California Aryan Brotherhood (AB) proudly displays a Star of David tattoo on this arm, which represents his Jewish heritage.

Finally, it is necessary to understand that the only thing that makes criminal White Supremacist gangs or White Supremacy groups different from other gangs and STGs is their hatred for others based on their race or ethnic background. Understand that all gangs and STGs "hate" others for a variety of reasons including which neighborhood a person lives in. The difference with White Supremacist and White Supremacy groups is that society has deemed their brand of hate more offensive then the hate practiced by classic street gangs and STGs.

White Supremacist Groups, Gang and Security Threat Groups

1st SS Kavallerie Brigade Motorcycle Division
211 Crew
5150 (Female)
Atlantic City Skinheads (SH)
American Third Party
American Nazi Party
Arizona Boot Boys (SH)
Aryan Barbarian Brotherhood
Aryan Brotherhood
Aryan Circle
Aryan Family
Aryan Knights
Aryan Militant Party
Aryan Nation
Aryan Nation Revival
Aryan Nazi Brotherhood
Aryan Outlaws
Aryan Party
Aryan Republican Army
Aryan Syndicate
Aryan Terror Brigade
Aryan Warriors
Aryan Youth Movement
Blood and Honor
Boneheads (SH)
Boot Boys (SH)
British National Party
Brothers of White Strength
Brotherhood of Klans Knights of the KKK
California Skinheads
Combat 18 (SH)
Confederate Hammerskins
Connecticut White Wolves
Comrades of Our Racist Struggle
The Covenant, the Sword and the Arm of the Lord.
Creativity Alliance
Creativity Movement
Crew 38
Deadman Inc–United
Death Head Hooligans (SH)
Death Squad (SH)
Denver Skins
Dirty White Boys
Dixie Knights (KKK)
D.O.T.A.R. (Defenders of the Aryan Race)
E.S.W.P. (SH) (East Side White Pride)
Eastern Hammerskins
European Kindred
Hammerskins
Family Affiliated Irish Mafia
Fraternal White Knights of the KKK
Fourth Reich
Freedom 14 (SH)
Ghostface
Hammer Head Skins
Hard Ass Crackers
Hate Cops (SH)
Hoosier-State Skins
Indiana Outlaw Hammershins
Inland Empire Skinheads
Imperial Klans of America (KKK)
Iron Eagles (SH)
Keystone States Hammerskins
Ku Klux Klan (KKK)
Knights of the Nordic Order
Lakeside Gangsters (SH)
The Leaderless Resistance Movement
Lomita Village Gang (SH)
Low Life Club
Mile High Skinheads
Midland Hammerskins

Montana Creators Assembly
National Alliance
National Knights of the KKK
National Skinhead Front
National Vanguard
National Vastilian
Nationalist Movement (SH)
Nazi Low Riders
NSM (National Socialist Movement)
Neo-Nazi Skinheads
New Aryan Empire
North American Skinheads
North East White Pride (SH)
Northern Hammerskins
Norwegian Skins
Outlaw Hammerskins
Peckerwoods
PEN 1
Phineas Priesthood
Phoenix Bootboys
Posse Comitatus
P.O.W.A.R. (SH) (Preservation Of the White Aryan Race)
The Order
Sacto Skins (SH)
Saxon Knights
Silent Brotherhood
Silver State Skinheads
Silent Aryan Warriors
Skinheads (SH)
Soldiers of Aryan Culture
SS Guardians
SS Knights (SH, KKK)
Strike Force (SH)
Supreme White Alliance
Supreme White Power
South African Afrikaner Resistance
South Jersey Skins
Southern Cross Hammerskins
Southern Knights of the KKK
Time Keepers
United Aryan Brotherhood
United Aryan Soldieries
United Brotherhood
United Brotherhood Kindred
United Klans of America
United Society of Aryan Skinheads
United White Knights of the KKK
United Northern and Southern Knights of the KKK
Vinland Hammerskins
Volksfront (SH)
W.A.S.P. (White Anglo Saxon Protestants)
W.A.R. (White Aryan Resistance)
WAR Skins
West Coast War Skins
Western Hammerskins
White Boy Society
White Patriot Party
White Pride
White Revolution
White Rule Union
White Wolves
Women for Aryan Unity
Woman of the KKK
The Wood Pile
Working Class Skins
World Church of the Creator

* SH = Skinhead membership
* KKK = Ku Klux Klan membership

Non-Racist Skinheads

A.R.A. (Anti-Racist Action)
FSU (Friends Stand United, Fucking Shit Up)
Gay and Lesbian Skinheads
G.S.G. (Gay Skinhead Group)
S.H.A.R.P.s (Skinheads Against Racial Prejudice)
Skinheads for Christ
Socialist Skinheads
Trojan Skinheads
Traditional Skinheads

White Supremacist Tattoos, Symbols, Graffiti, and Marks

KKK

14 Words

Hail Hitler

Nazi SS Bolts

Aryan Brotherhood

Blood and Honor

Swastika

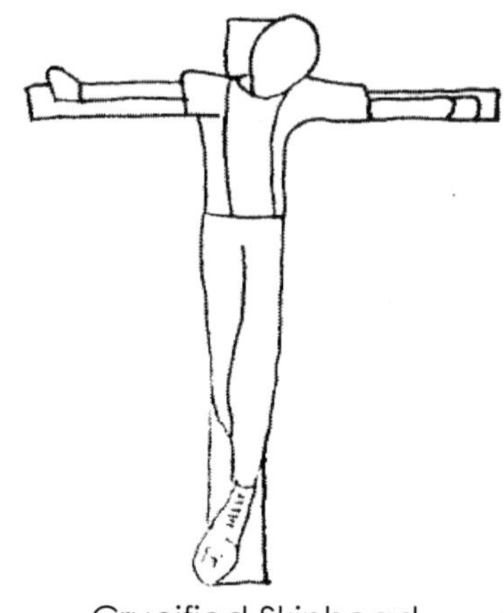

Crucified Skinhead

Clover (3 or 4 leaf)

3/11

KKK

Peckerwood	Featherwood
Woodpile	White Power
White Pride	Aryan Pride

Skinhead Boot Lace Codes and Symbolism

Color of Laces	Meaning or Symbolism
Blue:	Cop killer
Green:	Celtic Pride, Environmentalist, S.H.A.R.P. or Homosexual Basher
Pink:	Homosexual skinhead
Red:	Nazi or the National Front, committed a homicide
White:	White Power or White Pride
Yellow:	Anarchy, Asian, Cop Basher, Ultra violent
Yellow, Black, and Blue:	S.H.A.R.P.

White Supremacist Terms and Acronyms

5 Words

Represents the sentence "I have nothing to say," which represents the "code of silence," which Alex Curtis, a White Supremacist leader in California, tells all members of the movement to invoke when confronted by law enforcement.

7, 14, 21

Represents the number of eyelets found in a person's Doc Martin boots.

14 Words

Represents the sentence "We must secure the existence of our people and a future for white children," which was taken from a speech by David Lane, a well known and respected leader within the White Supremacist movement. Lane died in Federal Prison on May 28, 2007.

18

Represents the first and the eighth letters of the alphabet "A" and "H." "A H" representing the words "Adolf Hitler."

23

Represents the twenty-third letter of the alphabet "W." "W" representing the word "White."

28

Represents the second and eighth letter of the alphabet, which are B and H, representing the words Blood and Honor.

83

Represents the eighth and third letters of the alphabet "H" and "C." "H C" representing the words "Hail Christ."

88

Represents the eighth letter of the alphabet "H," "H H" representing the words "Hail Hitler."

100%

Represents a person who believes they are "Pure Aryan or has pure white roots."

211 Crew

211 refers to the California penal code for Armed Robbery. Although originally formed as a non-racist, Irish Pride Prison gang in Colorado, the 211 Crew has quickly become predominantly made up of White racist inmates.

3 / 11 or 311

The 3 refers to 11 three times. The 11 represents the eleventh letter of the alphabet "K" or in other words 311 represent the letters KKK meaning Ku Klux Klan.

4/19

Represents the date "April 19." April 19 is the anniversary date of the end of the Waco, Texas, Branch Davidians standoff in 1993 and the anniversary of the Oklahoma City bombing in 1995.

4/20

Represents the date "April 20." April 20th is celebrated by White Supremacists as Adolf Hitler's birthday. 420 or the time 4:20 is also said to be the time when people are supposed to get high on marijuana throughout the world. The term "420 world wide" is often used by "pot heads."

666

Is a biblical reference to the "mark of the beast." The number "666" is also used to symbolize Satan and evil.

Down with the Sickness

Means they are a 211 Crew Member

Featherwood

A term used to describe a female member of the Peckerwood gang.

Hep C +

This phrase means an individual is down with the sickness, meaning they are a 211 Crew member or associate.

N A E

Represents the phrase "New Aryan Enforcer"

Peckerwood or Wood

The term Peckerwood or "wood" is a slang term coined in the California Department of Corrections by non-White inmates, used to refer to White inmates. The term quickly caught on with White prison gangs and now normally refers to a White Supremacist. Although there is a White Supremacist group called the Peckerwoods, the term generally refers to any White Supremacist it does not mean that the person using that term is a member of the Peckerwood gang.

P O W E R

Represents the phrase "Preservation Of the White Aryan Race."

S A C

Represents the phrase "Soldiers of Aryan Culture."

Skin City

Refers to the city of Portland, Oregon, which is viewed by White Supremacists as a safe haven.

WAR (W.A.R.)

Represents the phrase "White Aryan Resistance."

W.A.S.P.

Represents the phrase "White Anglo Saxon Protestants."

Woodpile

Refers to Peckerwood associates who have not served a prison sentence.

The History of Skinheads

Skinhead Movement

The skinhead movement is perhaps one of the most misunderstood cultural developments in modern time. Although there are many racist groups of skinheads throughout the country, such as the Hammerskins, there are many non-racist skinhead groups as well. Groups like the Skinheads Against Racial Prejudice or S.H.A.R.P.s and the Straight Edge(rs) make up two of the largest non-racist skinhead groups in the country. Even with the differences between these groups, all of these groups offer a unique situation to law enforcement and a common history dating to the 1960s.

SKINHEADS (WHITE SUPREMACIST AND NON-SUPREMACIST)

Type of Gang: Non-traditional

Founded: 1960s in Great Britain

Founded by: By middle and lower class young adults who pride themselves on being working class and where offended by the Modernists or the MOD movement.

General racial makeup: Caucasian and non-African Americans

Main rivals: Other groups and African-Americans

Major historical events:

Began as a workers' rights socialist group.

1960s—adopted the clothing of the dock workers of the time, i.e., shaved heads, steel-toed boots, and suspenders known as braces.

1960s—the shaved heads of skinhead members led to members being referred to as skinheads.

1970s—British National Party begins to recruit members of Skinheads leading to the creation of the White Supremacist Skinhead.

1970s—an influx of West India immigrants enter the United Kingdom leading to an immigration backlash.

1970s—the Anti-Paki League or APL was created. Members of the British National Party begin to join the APL. The "bashing" of homosexuals and immigrants becomes a favorite past time of racist skinheads.

1970 to present—both racist and non-racist skinheads spread throughout the world.

1970 to present—racist groups such as "WAR" and the National Alliance attempt to recruit and organize skinhead groups.

Early 1980s—the Hammerskins are formed in the United States with the goal of organizing racist skinheads groups into one group with a shared goal and philosophy.

The History of the 211 Crew

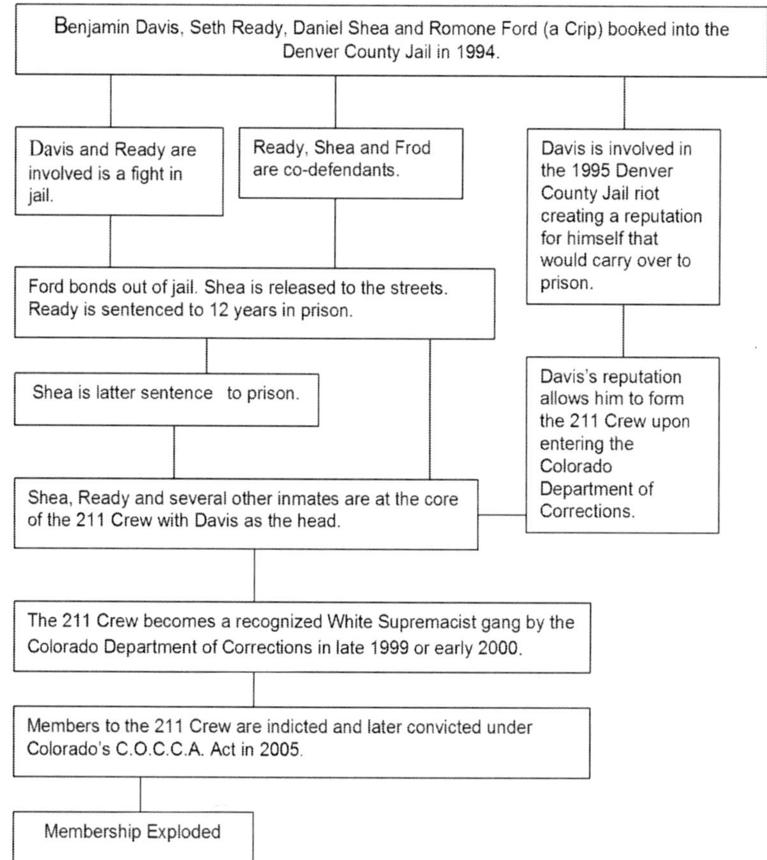

Note: Because of the media coverage of the 211 Crew trials in 2005 and the sentencing of its leadership to long prison sentences, the 211 Crew has grown within the Colorado Department of Corrections. The impact of this "boom" in membership is yet to be fully realized.

General Aryan Brotherhood Hierarchy

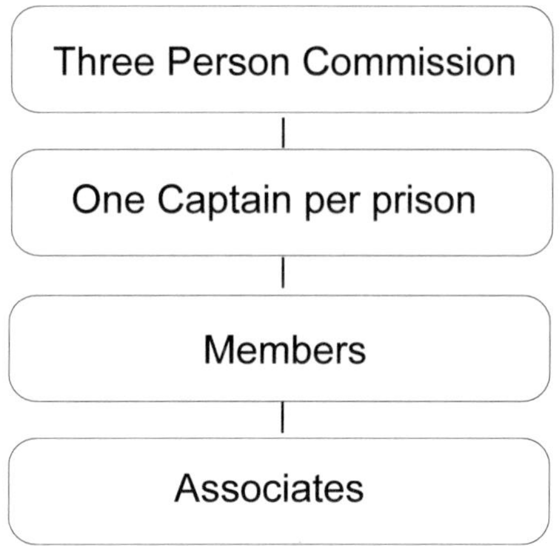

At the current time it is not clear how many facilities have branches of the Aryan Brotherhood within the California, Federal, and other Departments of Corrections.

211 Crew Hierarchy (2004 and 2008)

(Possible Chain of Command 2004 – 2008)

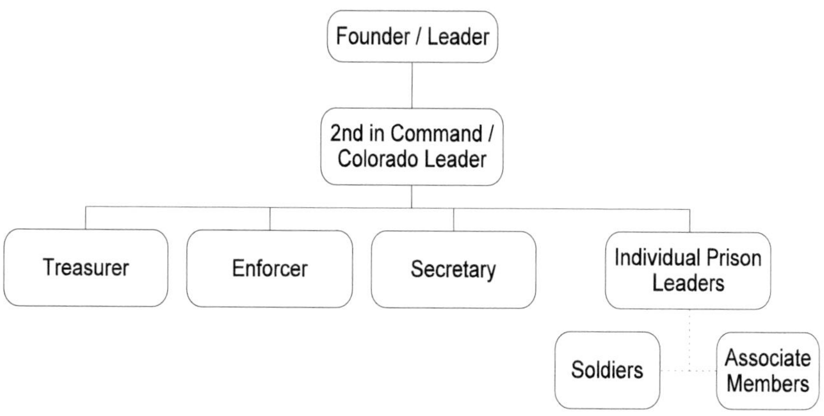

(Possible Chain of Command as of 2008)

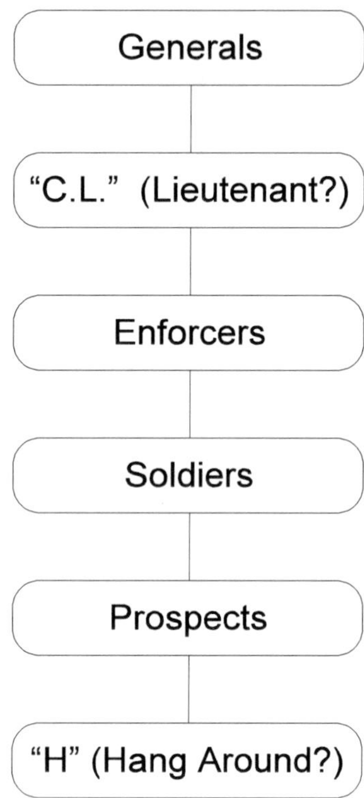

General Ku Klux Klan Hierarchy

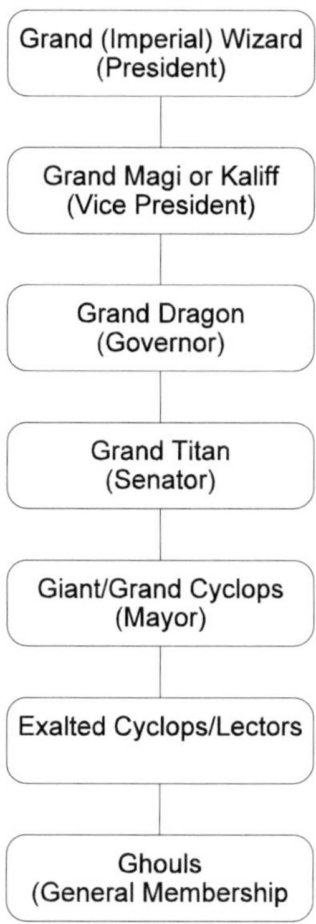

The above hierarchy is a general KKK hierarchy that is used by several different KKK style groups throughout the United States. Some KKK groups have changed the titles of some of the positions, but the general responsibility of each position remains the same.

European Kindred Hierarchy (Prison Model)

European Kindred Hierarchy (Street Model)

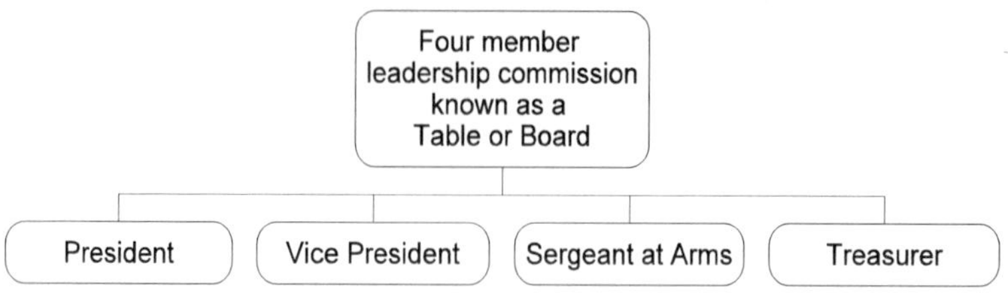

The White Supremacist Calendar

January 15	Martin Luther King's birthday (protested)
January 16	Robert Mathew's birthday (founder of "The Order")
January 30	Nazi Party came into power in Germany (1933)
February 2	Vala's Vision or Maidens Day (Odinizm)
February 6	Members of "The Order" are sentenced to prison (1986)
February 18	Aryan Women League is founded (1989)
March 2	David Lynch killed in his home (leader of National Front and Sacto Skins)
March 9	George Lincoln Rockwell's birthday (founder of the American Nazi Party)
March 21	Spring Evenight (Odinizm)
April 4	Martin Luther King Jr. assassinated (1968)
April 19	Oklahoma City Bombing by Timothy McVeigh (1995); Raid on the Branch Davidians in Waco, Texas by the FBI (1993)
April 20	Adolph Hitler's birthday; Columbine High School Shooting (1999)
April 26	Rudolf Hess's birthday (Hitler's Deputy Führer); Confederate Memorial Day; and Israel Independence Day (protested)
May 1	Walpurgia Feast or May Eve (Odinizm)
May 6	KKK incorporates in 1866
May 28	David Lane dies in Federal prison (2007)
June 2	Timothy McVeigh is convicted for the Oklahoma City bombing (1997)
June 3	Jefferson Davis' birthday (President of the Provisional [Confederacy] Government from November 6 1861 until his capture May 9, 1865)
June 6	Tom Metzger, leader of WAR, wins the congressional primary (1980)
June 11	Timothy McVeigh is executed in Federal Prison (2001)
June 13	Timothy McVeigh is sentenced to death (1997)

June 21	Summer Sunstead (Odinizm)
July 4	Independence Day. Celebrated as Revolution Day by White Supremacists
July 13	Nathan Bedford Forrest's birthday (1821, the Ku Klux Klan founder)
July 23	William Pierce, author of the *Turner Diaries* and leader of the National Alliance, dies (2002)
August 1	Hloaf Festival, Lammas (Odinizm)
August 20	Huey Long's birthday (Neo-Nazi)
September 2	Settler's Day in South Africa
September 8	Pastor Richard Butler, leader of the Aryan Nation, dies (2004)
September 15	National Aryan "POW" Awareness Day
September 21 (Approximately)	Fall Evenight, Harvest (Odinizm)
September 22	"The Order" is founded, early 1980s
October 24	Tom Metzger, leader of WAR, is convicted in Portland, Oregon (1990)
October 31	The Night of Specters (Odinizm)
November 9 & 10	Kristallnacht or Crystal Night (1938)
November 11	Heroes' Day (Odinizm)
December 8	Robert Mathews, leader of The Order, stands off with the FBI at Whidbey Island, National Martyrs Day
December 24	The Ku Klux Klan is founded (1865)
December 21, 24, 25, 31; Jan. 1 & 2	Winter Sunstead and Yule (Odinizm)

Introduction

Sadly, so-called Graffiti Krews (Crews) or Tagging Krews (Crews) are generally not categorized by law enforcement as a gang or security threat group because they are often made up of gang members from different gangs and are not involved in "gang activity." This assessment flies in the face of reason and lacks any real credibility when you apply the definition of a gang provided in this text or for that matter any other definition. When you apply the definition of a gang to Tagging/Graffiti Crews you will discover that they are, in fact, gangs. Furthermore, most Tagging/ Graffiti Crews do hundreds of thousands, if not millions, of dollars of damage a year. Most people would be hard pressed to point to a gang or STG that is allowed to do that much damage and is still considered by law enforcement to be more of a nuisance then a criminal group. For these reasons, and the "evolution of Tagging Crews" discussed in this chapter, the following information has been included.

Tagging Crews

Tagging crews normally identify themselves by initials rather than by name. The meaning of the initials can change on a regular basis as each group's members individually see fit. It is common for tagging crews to be made up of individuals who are gang and non-gang members. It is also common to find members of different gangs within the same tagging crew. The reason for this unique mix of gang and non-gang members in a tagging crew is because the purpose of a tagging crew is the "hanging" of "art," or "graffiti," as opposed to an organized gang-style activity. Tagging crews organizational design runs the gamut, from very organized to loosely organized. The following picture is an example of a "Tagger," who included the name of his tagging crew "RTD" (middle right of picture) and his street gang "OX3" (Oldies 13) (lower left of picture).

The following list contains examples of local and national tagging crews and the reported meaning(s) of each set of initials. In some cases, there are multiple reported meanings for each set of initials.

ABC: Always Bombin Crew
ABS: Always Bombin Society
ABS: Absolute Kings
ACC: All Criminal Crew, Another City Conquered, Another Criminal Chased
ACK: Aerocol Combat Krew
ADB: Always Dropping Bombs
ADK: After Dark Krew
AE: Alter Ego
AFC: Art Fiends Crew
AFK: Art Fiends Krew
AM: Always Mobbin
AOM: Army of Minds
AR: Artistic Resistance
AOK: All Out Kings
AOM: All Out Mobbin
ANL: Aztec Nation Locos
ARC: Artists Reppin Colorado
ASE: All Stars Elite
ATF: Active Taggers Federation
ATU: Always Taggin Up
AWS: Artists With Style
AWT: All World Thugs
BCT: Boulder County Rasied
BCT: Brick City Thugs (Crip Associate)
BCK: Bombin Cold Knights
BDK: Beyond Death Kings
BOC: Bomber of Colorado
BSK: Blunt Session Kings
BTP: Bomb The Planet
BTK: Broom Town Killaz, Born To Kill, B-Town Killers
BTR: Burin The Rails
CHAK: Creating Hated Art Krew
CIA: Criminals In Action
CISK: Creeping In Silence Krew
CLK: Clown Love Kings
CREATURES: Creatures Crew
CRB: Castle Rock Bombers
CTA: Crime Trough Art

CVK: City Vandals Krew
CWD: Crazy World Devils
DBS: Denver Bomb Squad
DCB: Denver City Bombers
DCK: Destroying Crews Konstantly
DCT: Denver City Thugs
DE: Denver Elite
DF: Doin Freight
DFK: Denver's Finest Krew
DHS(K): Denver Hit Squad, Doin Hot Shit Kings
DIA: Doin Insane Ary
DIAK: Down In Action Krew
DIE: Die Eternally, Death In Effect, Destined to Eternity
DK: Dark Knights
DMK: Dark Magic Kings
DMK: Dark Mined Kings
DTK: Denver True Kings
DTK: Down To Kill
DOA: Disciples of Aerosol
DOC: Denver Organized Crime
DRUG: Denvers Real Under Ground
DSK: Dark Side Knights, Dope Smoking Krew, Dope Smoking Kids
DVS: Denver Vandal Squad
ECK: Evil Chcano Kings
EK: Englewood Killas
ELK: Ever Lasting Kaos
EMC: Equal Member Crew
EMS: Envy My Style / Evil Minded Soldiers (Sureno 13 ties)
EOS: Envy Our Style
ETK: Emerging Talent Krew
EV: Everlasting Vandals
EWJ: Englewood's Wickedest Juggalos
FTK: Fuck the Kops
FTP: Fuck The Pigs
GAM: Guerilla Art Movement
GF(K): Getting Famous Krew, Getting Fucked Krew (South Side)
GTK: Grim Team Kings
GTP: Gangster True Preps
GSK: God Sent Krew
GSK: Goons Squad Krew
HBK: Hit a Bitch Krew
HCSK: High Class Serial Killers
HDK: Half Dead Killaz (Juggalos)
HK: Hells Kids
HLC: High Life Crew
HMP: Hit Man Posse
H8R: Hater Crew
HWS: Hitting Wit Style
IBC: International Bombing Crew
IMK: Insane Mobstaz
INS: Insane Notorious Scribblers
KD: Kings Destroy
KEA: Killin Em All
KEO: Killing Em All
KH: Kinky Hoes
KHT: Kan't Handle This
KMC: Kausin Mass Controversy, Kreative Minds Concur
KNO: Kings No Other
KOA: Kings of Art
KOC: Kings of Colorado (NSM ties)
KOH: Klutchin Our Heat, King Of Highways.

KOS: Knocking Out Suckas, Kriminals Out Shooting.
KR(A): Keep Reloading Ammo
KS: Kant Stop
KSK: Kan't Stop Kaos
KSM: Kan't Stop Me, Kan't Stop Mob, Krasy Style Mob, Killing Snitches Mob
KTR: Killing The Rest
KUV: Kaked Up Vandals
KYS(M): Know Your Style, Killing Your Style Mob, Keeping Sluts Moist (GKI ties)
LIFE Crew: Living in Full Effect
L2K: Love 2 Kill
LTK: Love To Kill
MHK: Most Hated Kings
MHS: Mile High Soldiers
MDK: Mexican Disciple Kings
MDR: My Daily Routine
MSK: Maniac Strap Killers, Mad Society Kings, Money Staking Kings, Mexican Style Kings, Money Sex Killers (NSM ties)
MTK: Mexicans Taking Control, Made to Kill.
NIC: No Identity Crew (Juggalos)
NGK: New Graffiti Kings
NIK: Now I Kill
NSC: North Side Crew
NSK: New Style Krew
NVK: North Valley Kings, Night Vandal Kings
OAK: On A Quest
OHF: One Happy Family
OKW: Our Krasy World, Out Kast Writers, Our Krus Wicked (GKI ties)
OMK: Open Minded Kings
OPK: Out Phor Kash
PBK: Pretty Boy Krew
PDK: Panty Dropper Krew (GKI ties)
PMC: Players Mobbin Crew
RAK: Real Art Kings
REK: Runnin Every Korner
RGK: Renown Graffix Kinigs Royally Getting Krowned
RHK: Raw Hittin Krew
RMS: Runnin Milehigh Streets
RRS: Real Rasta Style
RSB: Real Street Bombers
RSK: Runnin Shit Krew
RTD: Ready To Destroy, Roof Top Destroyers (National)
RTS: Running The Show
RWS: Real West Side (Blood ties)
SA(K): Street Assassins Krew (West Side)
SBK: Styles Beyond Kontrol
SHITK: Shit Krew
SK: Style Knights, Street Kings, Style Kings
SKA: Still Kicking Ass
SR: Satan's Rejects
SSK: Sprayin Street Konstantly
SLUTS: Stop Livin Up To Society
SMK: Single Minded Kulture / Sick Minded Kids
SWK: South West Kids
SWKK: South West Killa Klownz
SWS: Spraying with Style, Strong Writers Survive, Sick With Style, Sun Will Shine
SYK: Stomp Your Krew
TCA: The Con Artists
TCP: Taking Crews Potential

TDK: Tipin Down Klick, Taken Denver Krown, Trippen Down Kings, Tipin Down Kings
THC: The Habitual Criminals
TK: Truest Kings
TKO: The Knight Owls; Trust Know One; Technical Knock Out; The Krazy Ones; TaKing Over; Total Kaos (National)
TNC: Top Knotch Crew
TWC: The Wrong Crowd, Taking Without Consent
TWGK: The World's Greatest Krew
TWK: Third World Kings
TWO: Takin Whats Ours
TYK: Thought You Knew
UGL: Urban Graffiti Legends
USK: United Street Kings
UTI(K): Under the Influence (Krew)
VK: Vandyke Krew
VRM: Vandalizing Ruleless Minds
VTK: Vandal Incorporated Kings
WCK: We Criminal Regardless
WEC: Wreckin Every Crew
WFU: World Famous Underground
WK(S) (DUB K): World Kings (Soldiers), Wrecking Krew, Wicked Kings (GKI ties)
WM: West Mafia, Worlds Mine, West Side Mafia
WNC: West Niners Crew (GKI ties)
WOT: We On Top
WRK: World Reckin Krew
WRS: We Rek Shit
WSK: Wild Style Kings
WSM: West Side Mafia

The Evolution of Graffiti Crews

Nationally, graffiti crews typically evolve from a single individual, to a loosely associated group of individuals, to an organized graffiti crew, to an organized street gang. Due to the fact that graffiti or tagging crews are involved in ongoing criminal activity, mainly the graffiti itself, and they are a loosely knit group of taggers, they fall within the legal definition of a "gang." Generally speaking, it is not until a tagging crew becomes involved in more typical gang activity such as drive-by shootings, robberies, or drug dealing that they become classified as a "gang" by law enforcement, even though they meet the definition of a gang much earlier in their existence.

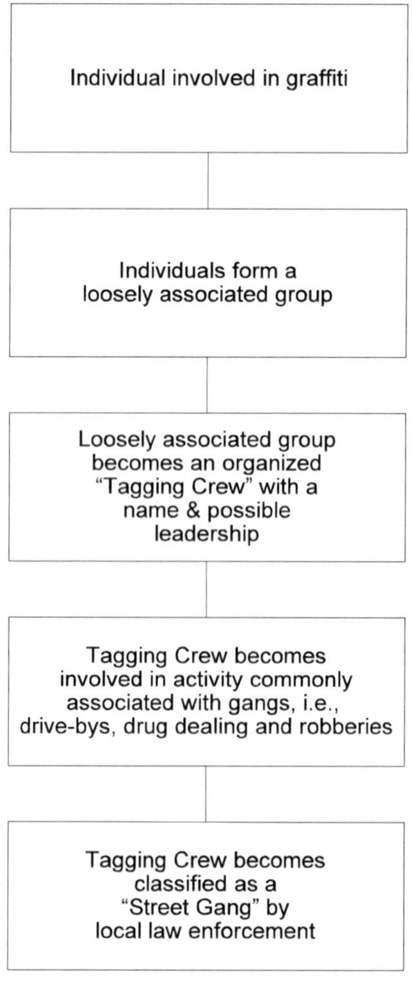

National Tagging Crew Hierarchy

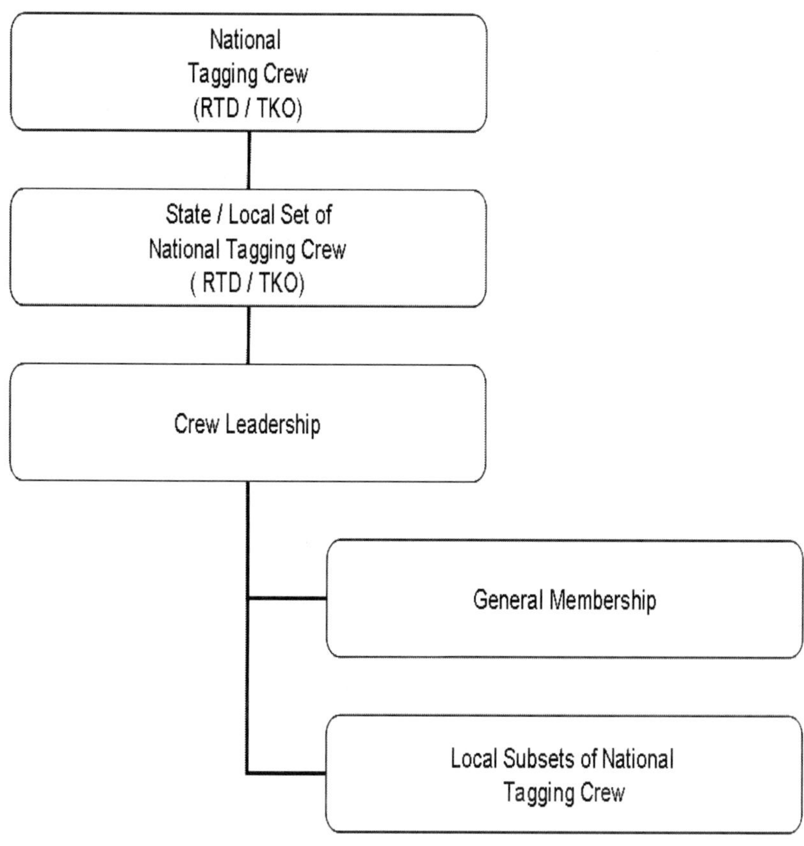

Introduction

This section contains information on gangs, security threat groups, and other groups that do not fit into the general categories discussed in the preceding pages.

Organized Crime Families Cartels

14 K Triads
Amezcua-Contreras Cartel
Amur River Society
Arellano Felix Organization
Beltran Leyva Organization
Bing Kong Tong
Black Dragon Triad
Black Poppy Triad
Blood Rose Triad
Bonanno Crime Family
Cali Cartel
Caro-Quintero Organization
Carrilo-Fuentes Organization
Cartel de Poiente
Cartel of the Millennium
Caruso Crime Family
Chicago Outfit
Colombo Crime Family
Colima Cartel
Coronel Villareal Organization
Cuong Hu Huynh Organization
DeCavalcante Family
Dixie Mafia
Eighty-Eight Triad
The Federation
Felix-Gallardo Origination
Flocc
Fontanna Crime Family
Fuk Ching Tong
Gambino Crime Family
Garduno Drug Family
Genovese Crime Family
Genyosha Society (Black Ocean)
Giglioti Crime Family
Golden Eye Triad
The Gran Familia
Greco Crime Family
Guadalajara Cartel
Gulf Cartel
Guzman Loera Organization
Hip Sing Tong
Hop Sing Tong
Hung Mun Tong
Inagawa-Kai Yakuza
Joaquin Guzman Loera
Juarez Cartel
La Cosa Nostra
La Familia
La Familia Michoacan
Leong Tong
Lombardi Crime Family

Los Zeta
Luchese Crime Family
Luen Kung Lok Triad
Juarez Cartel
Kam Lum Tong
Mascarenas Drug Family
Medellin Cartel
Melina Drug Family
Mexican Federation Cartel
New England Crime Family
North Valley Cartel
Nuero Laredo Cartel
Oaxaca Cartel
Octagon Triad
On Leong Tong
Patriaca Crime Family
Ricerche Crime Family
Samldone Crime Family
San Yee Triad
Scalise Family
Sinaloa Cartel
Sonora Cartel
Sumiyoshi-Rengo Yakuza
Sun Yee On Triad
Tijuana Cartel
Tung On Tong
Tsung Tsin Tong
United Bamboo
Valencia Cartel
Vicente Carrillo Fuentes Organization
Wo Hop To Triad
Yamaguchi-Gumi Yakuza
Yellow Lotus Trial
Zambada Garcia Organization

Italian-Style Organized Crime Hierarchy

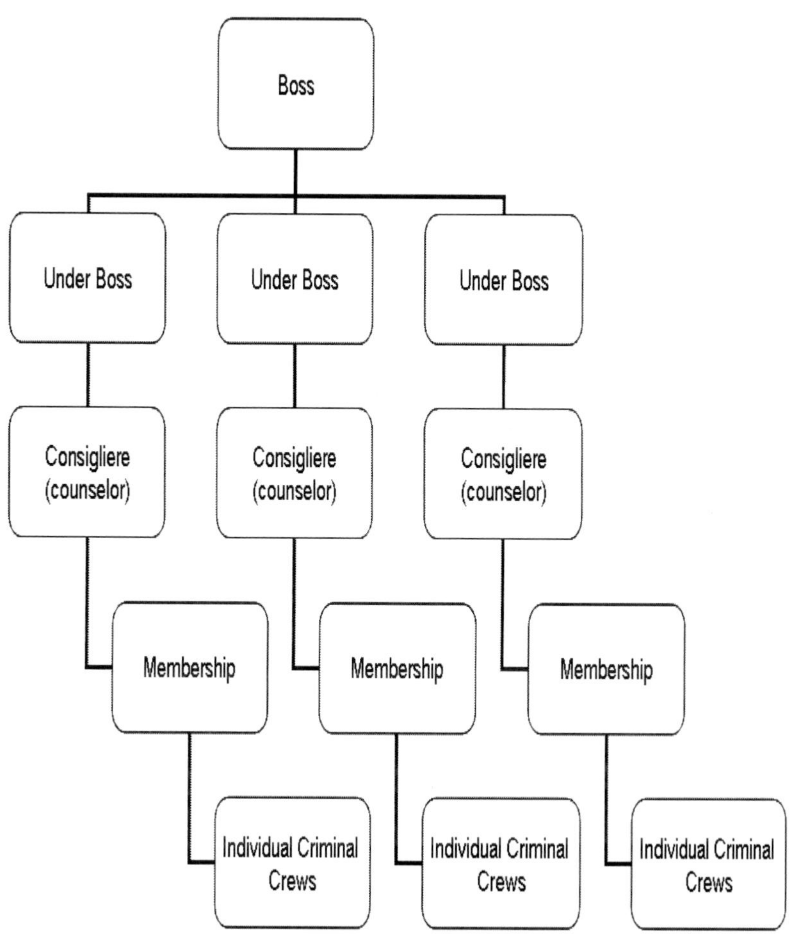

The Insane Clown Posse, a.k.a. ICP

The Insane Clown Posse (ICP) is a band that has a following similar to the Grateful Dead in the sense that the followers of ICP have their own identity; they call themselves Juggalos (males) or Juggalettes (female) in the same manner that Grateful Dead fans call themselves Deadheads. Additionally, like Grateful Dead fans, ICP fans have their own form of dress and are very dedicated and loyal to their music.

Although petty crime and drug crimes are always part of any subculture they are even more so when that subculture involves a transit population made up largely of teenagers and young adults with a limited income; however, there are those within the ICP subculture groups of Juggalos and Juggalettes who have taken this criminal element one step further and have become involved in "classic" street gang activities to include, but not limited to, narcotics activity, turf disputes with other gangs, weapons violations, auto theft rings, as well as other criminal endeavors.

The challenge to law enforcement has become to separate the criminal element from the law abiding music enthusiast. This task has proven very difficult because the Juggalos and Juggalettes who are law abiding and the ones who are not use the same symbolism and often dress in the same manner. Often, it is not until a criminal act or acts have taken place that a line can be drawn between the law abiding and criminal element.

The information contained in this section is not designed to enable you to make a distinction between law abiding and criminal Juggalos and Juggalettes, rather it is to allow you to simply identify them as Juggalos and Juggalettes. This is important because many Juggalos and Juggalettes have been misidentified and documented as Bloods and other gang members based on similar use of colors and symbols. Once a person as been identified as a Juggalo or a Juggalette, further investigation is needed to determine if they are in fact involved in criminal activity or are simply music lovers.

Insane Clown Posse Symbols

Hatchet Girl

Hatchet Man

ICP

Insane Clown Posse

Detroit-based Soda

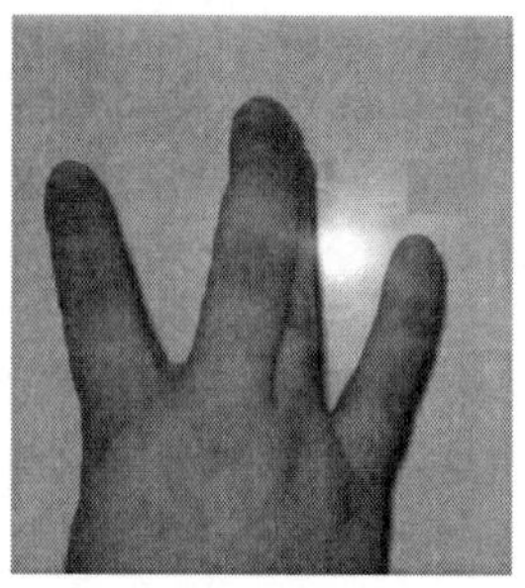

Wickedest

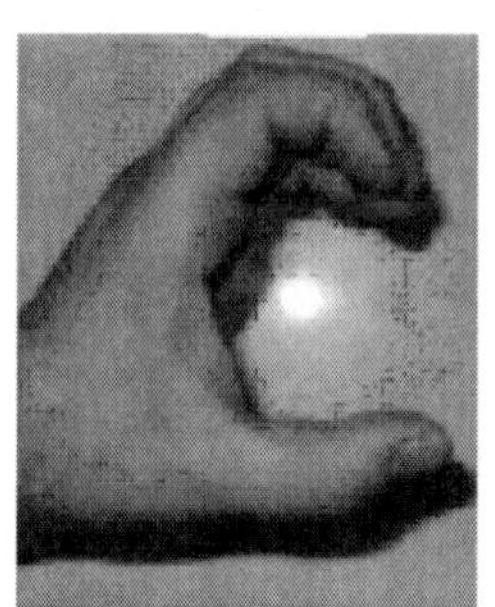

Clowns

ICP Division and Transition

Music Enthusiast vs. Criminal Activity and Gang Activity

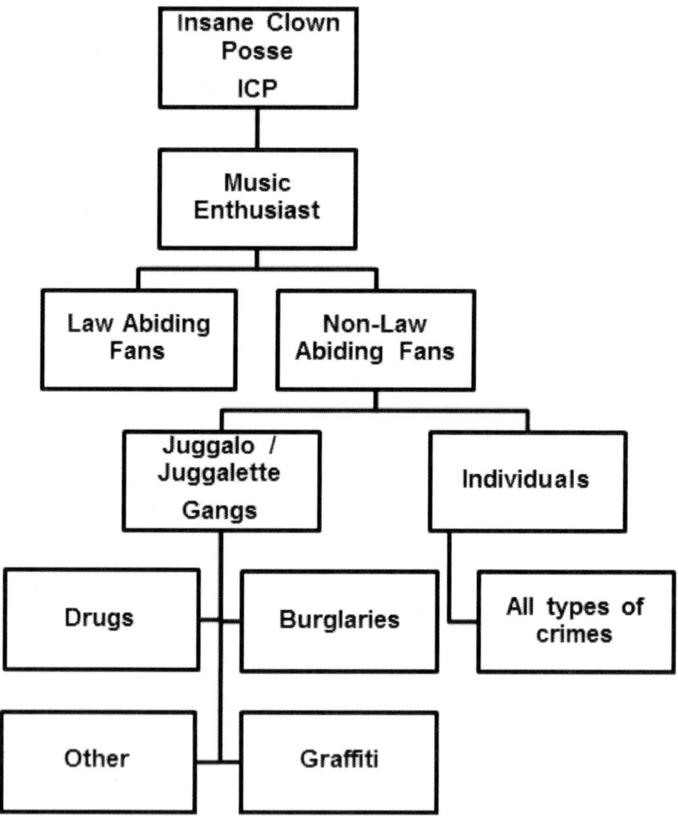

Insane Clown Posse History

INSANE CLOWN POSSE
"ICP" "WICKEDEST CLOWNS"

Type of Gang: Non-traditional (when functioning as a gang)

Founded: Early 1990, Psychopathic Records, Detroit, Michigan

Founded by: Joseph Frank "Violent J" Bruce and Joseph "Shaggy 2 Dope" Utsler

General racial makeup: All

Major historical events:

At least one of the ICP founder has a history in street gang activity.

ICP followers began calling themselves Juggalos and Juggalettes in 1992.

ICP won several music awards.

ICP has sold over 5 million records.

Late 1990s—some Local law enforcement agencies attempt to have some Juggalo and Juggalette groups categorized as street gangs due to ongoing street gang activity by subsections of the overall Juggalo / Juggalete subculture.

Left Wing Extremist and Disruptive Groups

Animal Defense League (ADL)
Animal Liberation Front (ALF)
Band of Mercy
Earth Liberation Front (ELF)
Hunt Saboteurs Association
North American Animal Liberation Front
Stop Huntingdon Animal Cruelty (SHAC)
The Family
Wild Earth Guardians
Win Animal Rights (War)
Primate Freedom Project

Dropout Gangs and Security Threat Groups

Two Fives or Deuce-Fives

Brothers by Choice (White Supremacist dropouts)

Gay Boy Gangsters (Homosexual dropouts)

Independent Riders

Northern Riders (Norteño 14 dropouts)

Note: Dropout gangs and STGs are made up of members of other gangs and STGs that have debriefed with law enforcement, informed, or others wise dropped out of a gang or STG. These dropout gangs and STGs began in the protective units of the California Department of Corrections as a way to protect each other from other inmates in protective custody as well as to victimize other inmates.

Native American Gangs and Security Threat Groups

The Boyz

Dine Pride (STG)

Indian Brotherhood

Indian Crips

Indian Posse

Indian Mafia

Manitoba Warriors

Native Gangster Bloods

Native Gangster Crips

Native Gangster Disciples

Nomads

Odd Squad

Red Nation Clique

Ruthless Deuce

TBZ

Warrior Society (STG)

The Wild Boyz

Youth Subcultures

Social-Based Subcultures

1. Skaters
2. Taggers
3. Sadomasochism (S&M)
4. BDSM (Bondage and Sadomasochism)
5. Goth
    a. Classic
    b. Modern
    c. Industrial

Religious-Based Subcultures

1. Wicca and other earth-based groups
2. Vampirism
3. Psychic Vampirism
4. Satanism
5. Paganism
6. Odenism and other Celtic-based groups
7. Witchcraft

Music-Based Groups

1. Techno and European Techno
2. Metal
3. Industrial
4. Ravers
5. Punk
6. Club Kids
7. Insane Clown Pose (ICP)
    a. Juggalos
    b. Juggalos (Criminal gang)
    c. Juggalettes
    d. Juggalettes (Criminal gang)

Political-Based Groups

1. Animal Rights
2. Ecosystem Preservation

3. Anti-War
4. Conservative and Liberal groups
5. Abortion Rights
   a. Pro-Life
   b. Pro-Choice

Membership in these groups or participation in one of the above groups or lifestyles does not necessarily suggest criminal activity. The above groups and lifestyles are often misunderstood or completely unknown to law enforcement and require familiarization to determine the true nature of many of these groups and lifestyles. It is not uncommon for criminals to be involved in the above lifestyles of groups even though the groups itself is not criminal in the same manner a poor business owner may be involved in the Better Business Bureau.

Introduction

All gangs and STGs in the United States use one form of codes/symbols or another. The two simplest forms of codes/symbols used by gangs and STG, and by far the most asked about, are hand signs, or signs as they are better known, and graffiti. As gangs and STGs became more sophisticated they required a way to communicate secretly with each other and with others in the criminal culture other than hand signs and graffiti. In order to do this, they developed their own written and verbal codes. The following are examples of the most common types of codes/symbols that are used by a variety of gangs and STGs in the United States. Gang and STG specific examples of symbols are located in the section dedicated to the gang or STG.

Common Gang Hand Signs

When considering hand signs its important to remember that most people do not communicate using hand signs. Therefore, anyone seen using hand signs to communicate with another person is likely to be a gang member (unless of course they are hearing impaired or an athlete in the middle of a game). It is also important to remember that hand signs change quickly and often. Keeping up with hand signs can be a very time consuming and futile process.

Because most hand signs are based on American Sign Language, there are common hand signs that are used by multiple gangs. For instance, gangs who affiliate themselves with the Crips use the hand gesture for the letter "C" found in American Sign Language (see photos that follow) even though they may be from different sets.

The use of American Sign Language by gang and STG members as a basis for their hand signs gives law enforcement a starting place when attempting to interpret hand signs. Although American Sign Language is used as a basis it is not strictly used, and therefore some hand signs are harder than others to interpret. The following examples of common hand signs are used by national gangs and STGs; some of which are clearly American Sign Language and some of which are more unique.

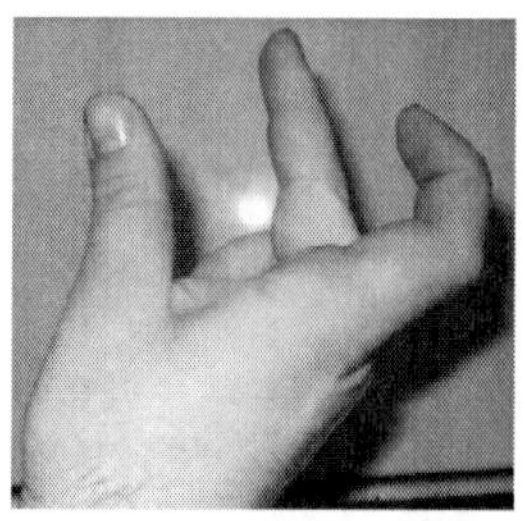

Folk Nation Pitchfork

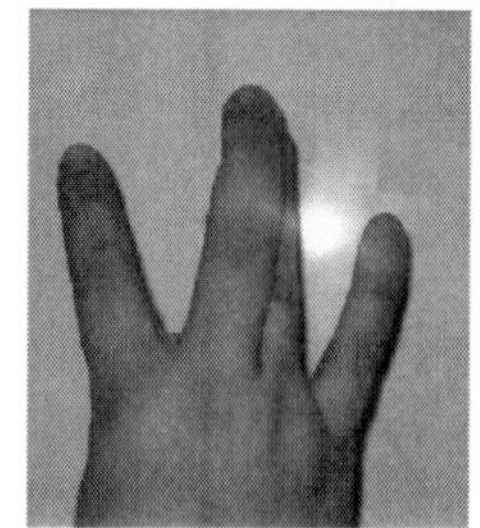

"W" or West Side

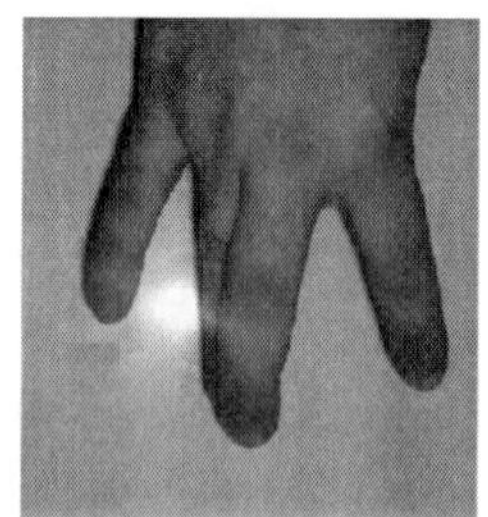

"M" or Mafia

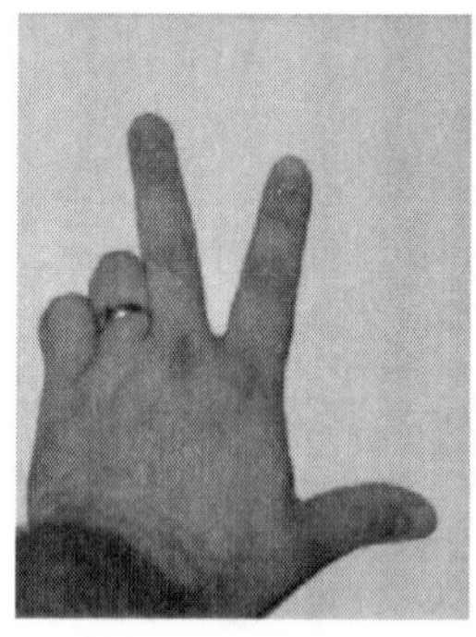

Vice Lords

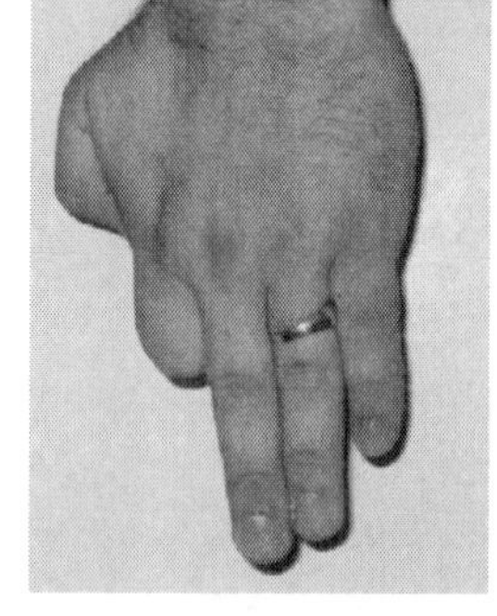

Piru

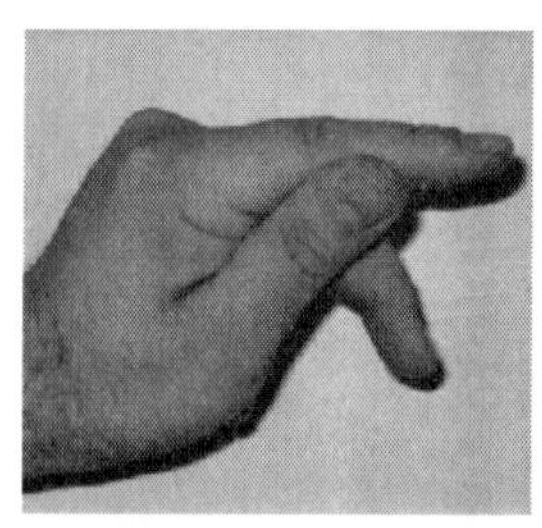

Kitchen Crips

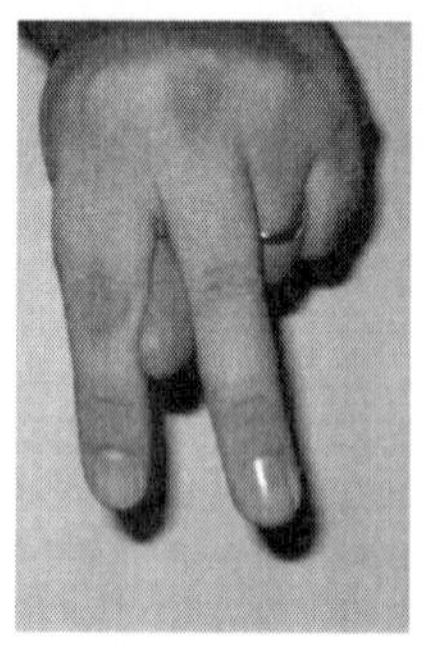

Hover Crips

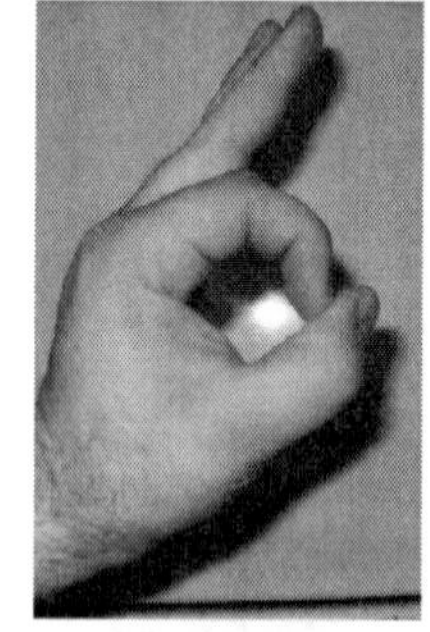

"B" or Blood

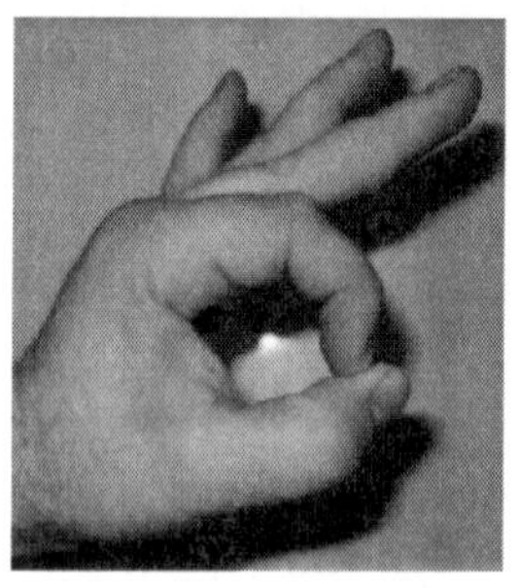

"BK" or Blood Killer

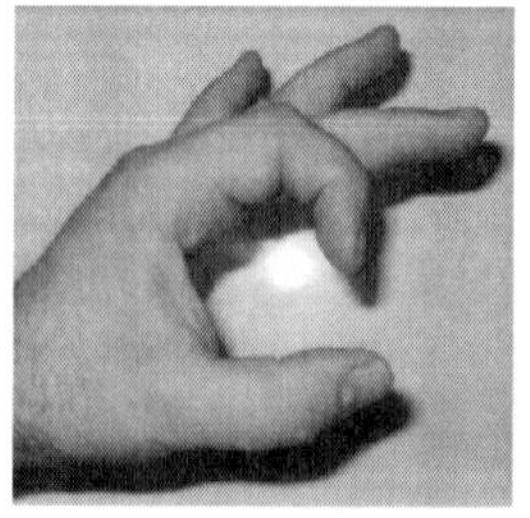

"CK" or Crip Killer

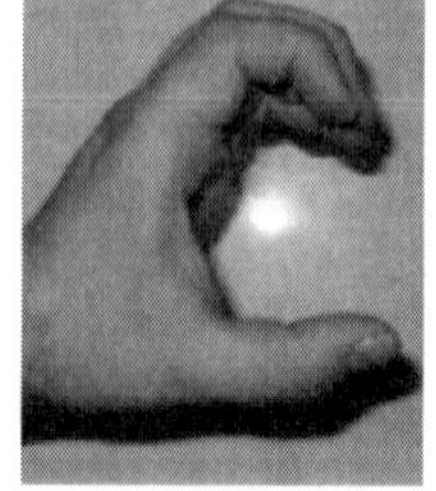

"C" or Crip

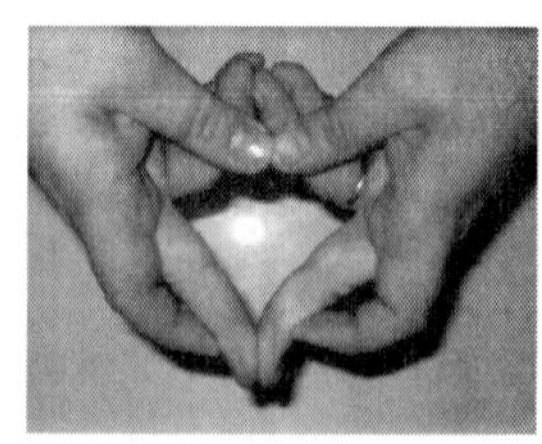

Six Point Star
of Folk Nation

Common Written Codes

Written codes are used by gangs and STGs for the same reason they are used by anybody: to stop third parties from understanding the message that is being communicated. The following are actual examples of codes that have been used by a wide variety of gangs and STGs nationally. Some of the codes may seem, and are in fact, juvenile; however, they are often overlooked by law enforcement officers. With each code there is information about where the code was discovered, if available. Also included are examples of coded messages.

The Numbered Alphabet

A	=	1	**N**	=	14
B	=	2	**O**	=	15
C	=	3	**P**	=	16
D	=	4	**Q**	=	17
E	=	5	**R**	=	18
F	=	6	**S**	=	19
G	=	7	**T**	=	20
H	=	8	**U**	=	21
I	=	9	**V**	=	22
J	=	10	**W**	=	23
K	=	11	**X**	=	24
L	=	12	**Y**	=	25
M	=	13	**Z**	=	26

This number code is created by numbering the letters of the alphabet. In the example above, the numbers of the alphabet began with the letter "A" for the sake of simplicity. Generally speaking, when numbers are used to represent a gang in their writings, tattoos, and graffiti they use this code, i.e., Border Brothers = B.B. or 22. In practice a code writer could start numbering the alphabet wherever the code writer wants (i.e., K = 1 L = 2) and so on. Please see the following examples:

Example 1:

Get rid of the car. =

7-5-20 18-9-4 15-6 20-8-5 3-1-18 or

75201894156208553118

Example 2:

Send me some money. =

19-5-14-4 13-5 19-15-13-5 13-15-14-5-25 or

19514413519151351315145 25

Example 3:

Pass message to Lil Pete. =

16-1-19-19 13-5-19-19-1-7-5 20-15 12-9-12 16-5-20-5 or

16119191351919175201512912165205

Example 4:

Two white ladies, three black ladies $500. =

20-23-15 23-8-9-20-5 12-1-4-9-5-19 20-8-18-5-5 2-12-1-3-11 12-14-9-5-19 or

2023152389205121495192081855212131112149519

Aztec Language of Nahuatl Code

Octli – Wine	Tototl – Bird	Ma Quixtiani – Teacher	Ceceppa – Repeat
Accotl – Sugar	Yoo Yoh – Warrior	Pilli – Prince	Tiein – What
Oceppa – Say again	Ixpol – Northern Indio	Canpol – Southern Indio	Lcalli – attack
cuachatl – shit	calmecac – school	pitzahuac – slim	ahuan – cellie
quenin – how	atle – nada	atl – water	atli – drink
ahuacatl – green	ollin – move	topile – cop	pal tloc pa – please
huehue – old wise man	tecichi – dog	ixtia – watch out	huarishi – coffee
zoqultl – brown	pitzome – pig	man – think	Itta – look
Inon – are	cua – food/eat	acualli – no good	chiua – doing
caqui – hear	anitla caqui – I can't hear	cualli – good	calli – house
nequi – want	caamo – no	quema – yes	qui – him/her
xos – the	nochipa – always	cihualt – woman	amesh – you
tlatoani – politician/warrior	mo – I	mopampa – for you	no pampa – for mi
titloc – with us	mo tloc – with you	no tloc – with me	tloc – with
cochi – sleep	cochia – sleeping	en – is	nica – I am
on – that	coatloxopeuh – powerful	tonantzin – our lady of guedalupe	Itech – have
timixtelotl – light	tuza – rat	tecpatl – tagger	tlilli – dark man
Iztapil – white man	Iztac – white/silver	teueome – neighbor	totonqui – hot
tiatoa – talk	temoa – says/saying	maca – give	techpa – respect
Ipal – thanks	tlazocamat – I appreciate	miec – much	amatl – piece of paper
amapi – message on paper	popoca – smoke	cualli ilhualli – good night	cualli ilhuitl – good day
cualli tewilli – good morning	ce – 1	ome – 2	yei – 3
nahui – 4	mawalli – 5	chicuace – 6	chicome – 7
chique yei – 8	chico nahui – 9	matlactli – 10	matlactli ce – 11
matlactli ome – 12	matlactli – yei – 13	matlactli nahui – 14	caxtlli – 15
caxtlli ce – 16	caxtlli ome – 17	caxtlli – yei – 18	caxtlli – nahui – 19

Source: Discovered by F.D.C. SeaTac intelligence program 2003

Example 1:

What good are you? =

ltta cualli inon amesh

Example 2:

Attack the cop. =

Lcalli xos topile

Example3:

I am with you. =

Nicu mo tloc

Example 4:

I thank you. =

Mo man amesh

Japanese Alphabet Code

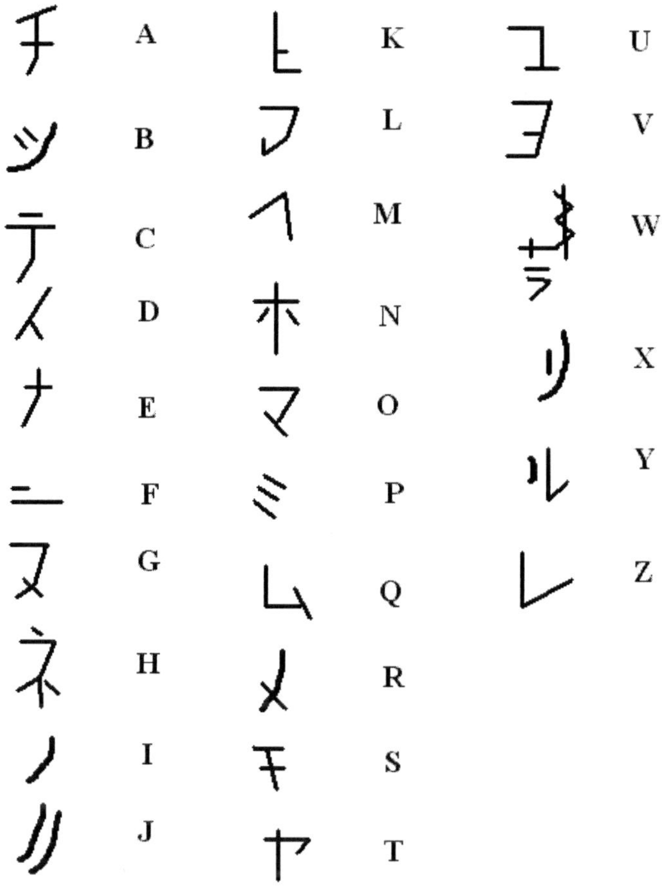

A	K	U
B	L	V
C	M	W
D	N	X
E	O	Y
F	P	Z
G	Q	
H	R	
I	S	
J	T	

Prior to the Colorado Department of Correction's discovery of the above code in the late 1990s/early 2000s, it was used by Sureño 13 gang members incarcerated in the Arkansas Valley Correctional Facility in Colorado. This code is believed to be a modified version of the Japanese alphabet. It is an example of how codes are created by modifying uncommon existing alphabet systems.

Example 1:

Kill the rat. =

Example 2:

Send drugs. =

Example 3:

Trust no one. =

Swahili Language Code

Swahili to English Translation

The Swahili language is a code that may be used by Blood gang members both inside and outside of prison. The use of the Swahili language by Blood gang members is believed to have originated in the correctional system as a way for inmates to avoid detection by correctional officers. The following are common examples of Swahili words used by gang members in both spoken and written communications.

A
Alhmisi = Thursday
Anza = Begin or Start
Arobaini = Forty
Asante = Thank you
Asari = Soldier

B
Badu = Still or Not Yet
Baya = Wrong
Bra = Beer
Bu Bu = Dumb
Bu Ria = Letter or Kite
Buluu = Blue
Burubara = Road
Bwana = Man / Mister

C
Chalewa = Holler
Chalewa = Later on
Changudoa = Prostitute
Cheza = Play
Chivi = Down
Chuna = Extortion

D
Da Da = Sister
Damu = Blood
Dawa = Medicine / Drugs
Duka = Shop

F
Fahamu = Understand
Feha = Money
Feisa = Police

G
Gari = Car

H
Habari = Hello
Hadari = Dangerous
Hakika = Real
Hakuna = There is not
Hamsini = Fifty
Hapana = No
Hatari = Danger
Hi Sho = This
Hujambo = How are you

I
Ijumaa = Friday
Ili Ili = Was
Ingl = Much
Ipi = Which
Ishirini = Twenty
Ita = Call

J
Jana = Yesterday
Janwani = Address

Jina = Name
Joto = Heat
Jumamosi = Saturday
Jumanne = Tuesday
Jumapili = Sunday
Jumatano = Wednesday
Jumatutu = Monday
Juu = Up

K
Kahawa = Coffee
Ke Le Le = Noise
Kesho = Tomorrow
Ki Dogo = Little
Kiasari = Like a Soldier
Kichumba = Cell
Kichunba Rafiki = Cellie
Kijafunza = Study
Kisho = Tomorrow
Kisu = Knife
Kiwe = Crazy or Rowdy Insane Pimp
Ku = To
Kubwa = Big
Kulia = Right
Kumi = Ten
Kuna = There is
Kupapasa = Feel
Kushoto = Left
Kusikuu = Tonight
Kutazama = Watch
Kutenda = Do
Kuwa = Kill
Kwaheri = Goodbye

L
La = No
La La = Sleep
Leo = Today
Lini = When
Lupango = Prison

M
Mahanda = Mexican
Mbaya = Bad
Mbili = Two
Mbule = Shit
Mfuko = Bag
Mguu Wa Kuku = Pistol
Mi Mi = I or Me
Mia = One hundred
Mibio Mchezd = Running Game
Mikanda = Strap
Mimi = I
Mjinga = Fool
Moja = One
Moshi = Smokes
Msaada = Help
Mto = Man
Mtoto = Youngster
Mwaka = Year
Mwana = Woman
Mwezi = Month
Mzunguwa Unya = Drug Dealer

N
Na = And
Nane = Eight
Nani = Who
Ndiyo = Yes
Nguruwe = Pig
Nia = Will
Nijibu = Answer Me
Nini = What
Nivisasa = Right Now
Njagu = Police
Nje = Out
Njema Oseibuli = Good Morning
Njema Usiki = Good Night
Njoo = Come
Noiyo = Yes
Nwezi = Comrade
Nyamaza = Be quiet

Nyekundu = Red
Nyeusi = Black
Nyumba = House
Nyupe = White
Nzuri = I'm fine

O
Ona = See
Ote = At

P
Pa = Give or Gave
Panya = Rat
Pata = Get or Got
Peleka = Send
Penye = At
Pesa = Money
Pia = Also
Pigana = Fight
Pigano = Battle
Polisi = Police
Pombe = Beer

R
Rafiki = Friend
Rafiki = Homie
Rafu = Long or Deep
Rangiya Ma Jani = Green
Rangiya Man Jano = Yellow
Runda Tundo = Asshole

S
Saba = Seven
Sasa = Now
Sawa Sawa = Right Right
Shikamou = Hello Sir or Ma'am
Sifahamu = Don't Understand
Sijambo = I'm Fine
Sijua = Don't Know
Sijui = I Don't Know
Sikaliza = Listen or Check Out
Siku = Day
Silaha = Weapon
Sisi = We
Sita = Six

T
Tabaka = Tier
Taka = Want
Tano = Five
Tatu = Three
Tazama = Look
Thelathini = Thirty
Tisa = Nine

U
Uke = Pussy
Upeuda = Love, Like or Loved One
Usalama = Security

V
Vipi = How
Vita = War

W
Wa = On
Wao = They
Wapi = Where
Watu = Our
Wazimu = Mad
Weupif = White Boy
Wewe = You
Wiki = Week
Wwe = Four

Y
Ye Ye = Him or He
Yeye = He or She

Z
Zuri = Beautiful

Coded Language Swahili

English to Swahili Translation

A
Address = Janwani
Also = Pia
And = Na
Answer Me = Nijibu
Asshole = Runda Tundo
At = Penye
At = Ote

B
Bad = Mbaya
Bag = Mfuko
Battle = Pigano
Be quiet = Nyamaza
Beautiful = Zuri
Beer = Bra
Beer = Pombe
Begin or Start = Anza
Big = Kubwa
Black = Nyeusi
Blood = Damu
Blue = Buluu

C
Call = Ita
Car = Gari
Cell = Kichumba
Cellie = Kichunba Rafiki
Coffee = Kahawa
Come = Njoo
Comrade = Nwezi
Crazy or Rowdy Insane Pimp = Kiwe

D
Danger = Hatari
Dangerous = Hadari
Day = Siku
Do = Kutenda
Don't Know = Sijua
Don't Understand = Sifahamu
Down = Chivi
Drug Dealer = Mzunguwa Unya
Dumb = Bu Bu

E
Eight = Nane
Extortion = Chuna

F
Feel = Kupapasa
Fifty = Hamsini
Fight = Pigana
Five = Tano
Fool = Mjinga
Forty = Arobaini
Four = Wwe
Friday = Ijumaa
Friend = Rafiki

G
Get or Got = Pata
Give or Gave = Pa
Good Morning = Njema Oseibuli
Good Night = Njema Usiki
Goodbye = Kwaheri
Green = Rangiya Ma Jani

H
He or She = Yeye
Heat = Joto
Hello = Habari
Hello Sir or Ma'am = Shikamou
Help = Msaada

Him or He = Ye Ye
Holler = Chalewa
Homie = Rafiki
House = Nyumba
How = Vipi
How are you = Hujambo

I
I = Mimi
I don't know = Sijui
I or Me = Mi Mi
I'm Fine = Nzuri
I'm Fine = Sijambo

K
Kill = Kuwa
Knife = Kisu

L
Later on = Chalewa
Left = Kushoto
Letter or Kite = Bu Ria
Like a Soldier = Kiasari
Listen or Check Out = Sikaliza
Little = Ki Dogo
Long or Deep = Rafu
Look = Tazama
Love, Like or Loved One = Upeuda

M
Mad = Wazimu
Man = Mto
Man / Mister = Bwana
Medicine / Drugs = Dawa
Mexican = Mahanda
Monday = Jumatutu
Money = Pesa
Money = Feha
Month = Mwezi
Much = Ingl

N
Name = Jina
Nine = Tisa
No = Hapana
No = La
Noise = Ke Le Le
Now = Sasa

O
On = Wa
One = Moja
One hundred = Mia
Our = Watu
Out = Nje

P
Pig = Nguruwe
Pistol = Mguu Wa Kuku
Play = Cheza
Police = Njagu
Police = Polisi
Police = Feisa
Prison = Lupango
Prostitute = Changudoa
Pussy = Uke

R
Rat = Panya
Real = Hakika
Red = Nyekundu
Right = Kulia
Right Now = Nivisasa
Right Right = Sawa Sawa
Road = Burubara
Running Game = Mibio Mchezd

S
Saturday = Jumamosi
Security = Usalama
See = Ona
Send = Peleka

Seven = Saba
Shit = Mbule
Shop = Duka
Sister = Da Da
Six = Sita
Sleep = La La
Smokes = Moshi
Soldier = Asari
Still or Not Yet = Badu
Strap = Mikanda
Study = Kijafunza
Sunday = Jumapili

T
Ten = Kumi
Thank you = Asante
There is = Kuna
There is not = Hakuna
They = Wao
Thirty = Thelathini
This = Hi Sho
Three = Tatu
Thursday = Alhmisi
Tier = Tabaka
To = Ku
Today = Leo
Tomorrow = Kisho
Tomorrow = Kesho
Tonight = Kusikuu
Tuesday = Jumanne
Twenty = Ishirini
Two = Mbili

U
Understand = Fahamu
Up = Juu

W
Want = Taka
War = Vita
Was = Ili Ili
Watch = Kutazama
We = Sisi
Weapon = Silaha
Wednesday = Jumatano
Week = Wiki
What = Nini
When = Lini
Where = Wapi
Which = Ipi
White = Nyupe
White Boy = Weupif
Who = Nani
Will = Nia
Woman = Mwana
Wrong = Baya

Y
Year = Mwaka
Yellow = Rangiya Man Jano
Yes = Ndiyo
Yes = Noiyo
Yesterday = Jana
You = Wewe
Youngster = Mtoto

Example 1:

Hello blood send kite now. =

Habari damu peleka bu ria sasa

Example 2:

When do they get out? =

Lini kutenda wao pata nje

Example 3:

What man was dangerous? =

Nin mto ili ili hadari

Example 4:

How are you friend? =

Hujambo rufiki

A Common Rune Alphabet and Numbers Translation

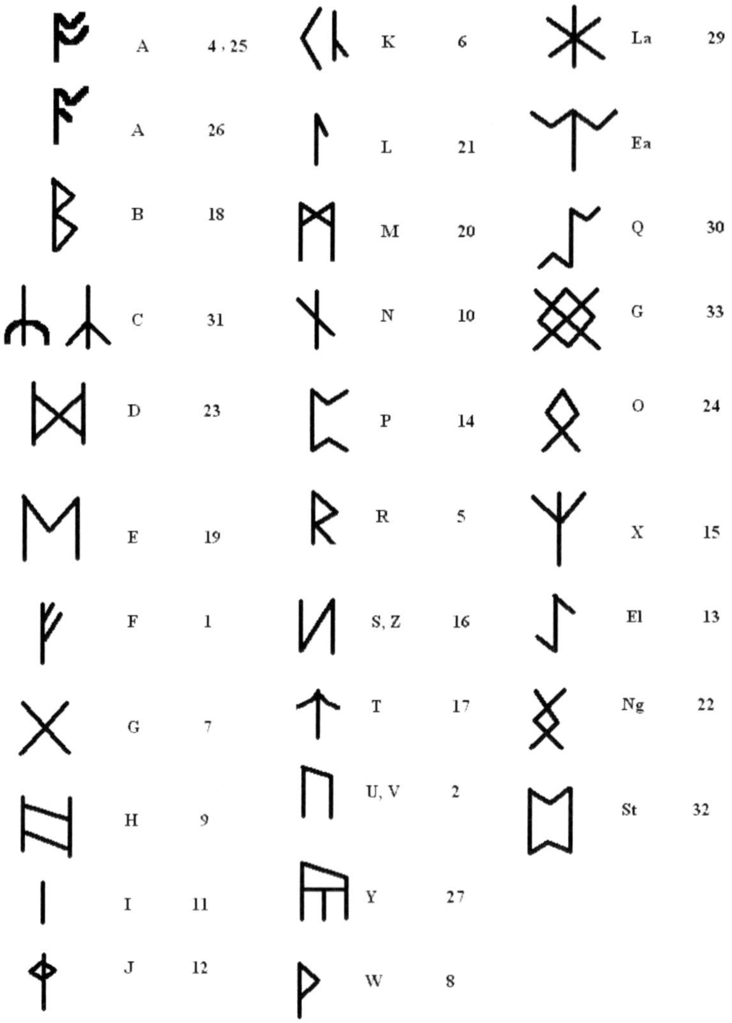

Letter	Number
A	4, 25
A	26
B	18
C	31
D	23
E	19
F	1
G	7
H	9
I	11
J	12
K	6
L	21
M	20
N	10
P	14
R	5
S, Z	16
T	17
U, V	2
Y	27
W	8
La	29
Ea	
Q	30
G	33
O	24
X	15
El	13
Ng	22
St	32

Runes are most commonly used by White and White Supremacist inmates. Many inmates will develop their own personal translation of runes requiring further decoding. The Rune translations previously shown are only examples. It is not uncommon for a message to be coded using a simple English code and then written in Rune form to further code the message.

Example 1:

Find some money. =

Example 2:

Who is the rat? =

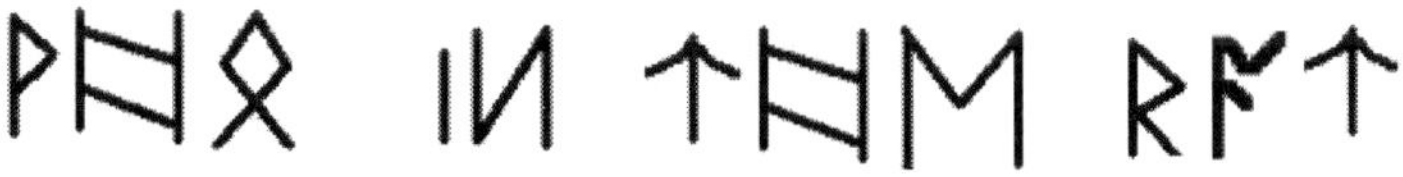

ᚹᚺᛟ ᛁᛋ ᛏᚺᛖ ᚱᚨᛏ

Example 3:

Is it clear? =

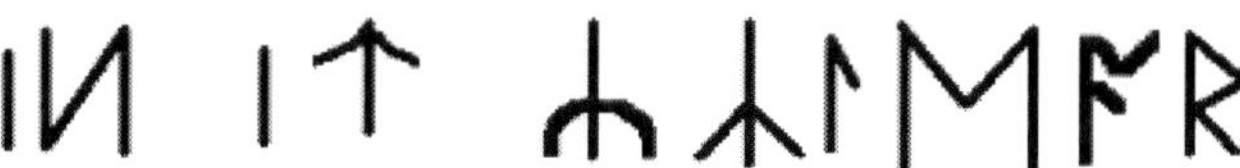

Tic Tac Toe Codes

Code 1

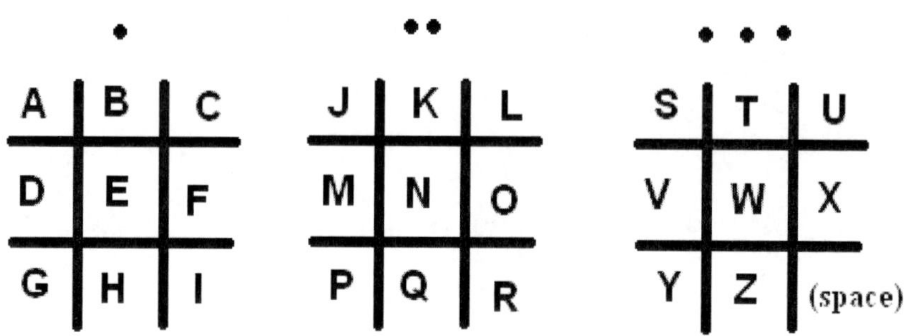

Code 2

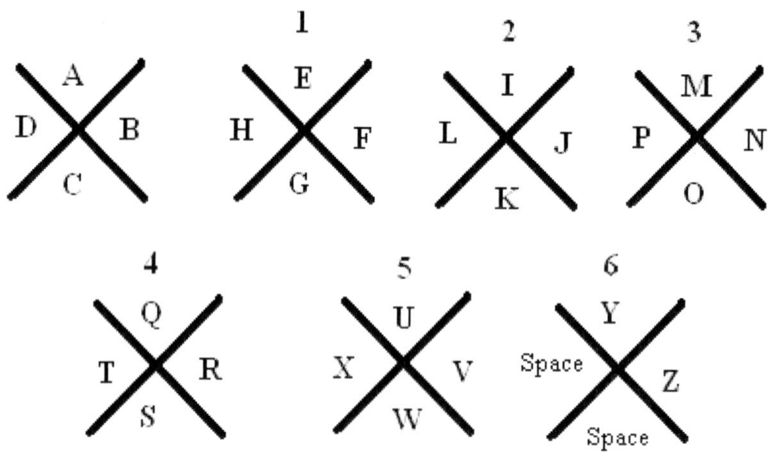

Example 1:

They call me Ted. =

Example 2:

What set do you claim? =

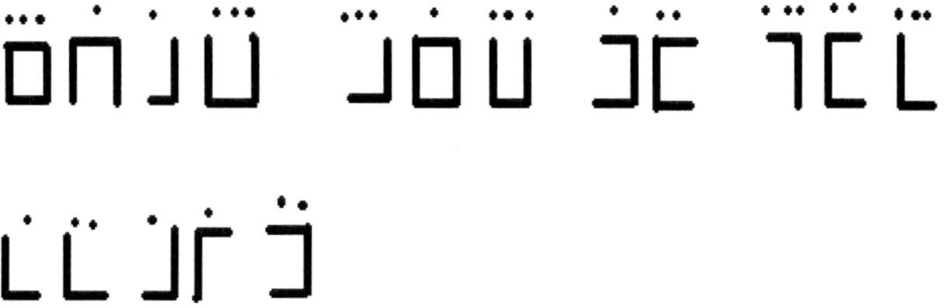

Example 3:

Sureño =

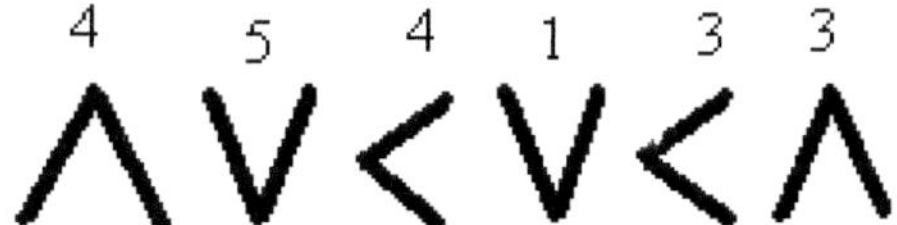

Coded Letters

Sometimes gang and STG members will not use a code to hide a message, rather, they will use the body of the letter to hide a message in plain sight. There are dozens of ways to hide messages in a letter but generally these types of letters involve using a "key" to determine which words in the body of the letter are used to form the hidden message.

Coded Example:

Sandra, *06/<u>10</u>/08*

Hey sweet heart what'z up? Not much here. If T-Bone comes by tell him I said what'z up. I'm out of here in MARCH! Yesterday I was sitting, thinking about you and me. I miss you so much! Your package of clothing got to me today. I thought I missed it. I can't wait to see you next week. It might be hard for you to get here with ice on the road. I thought that you could have T-Bone bring you. I can't wait for this all to end.

Love, Zig Zag

At first glance this letter looks very straightforward. Even if you read the entire letter, the letter still appears to be innocent in nature. The key to decoding the letter is found within the date. If you look at the date you will notice the ten is underlined. Due to the fact nothing else is underlined the writer wishes to draw attention to the ten making it the "key." To use the "key" you use every tenth word in the body of the letter. When every tenth word is read the message hidden in the letter starts to take shape.

The decoded copy of the above example follows with every tenth word in bold face and underlined.

Decoded Example:

Sandra, *06/<u>10</u>/08*

Hey sweet hart what'z up? Not much here. If ***T-Bone*** *comes by tell him I said what'z up. I'm* ***out*** *of here in MARCH! Yesterday I was sitting, thinking* ***about*** *you and me. I miss you so much! Your*

package *of clothing got to me today. I thought I* ***missed*** *it. I can't wait to see you next week.* ***It*** *might be hard for you to get here with* ***ice*** *on the road. I thought that you could have* ***T-Bone*** *bring you. I can't wait for this all to* ***end****.*

Love, Zig Zag

Decoded message:

T-Bone out. About package missed it. Ice T-bone. End (of message).

In this example, the hidden message becomes clear. In other cases the coding can be very complicated and in some cases can only be broken by professional code breakers if you do not have the key. Even with this said, it is important to keep in mind that most codes used by gang and security threat group members are simple. As an example, it is common for criminals in the Colorado Department of Corrections to refer to cocaine as "white woman" and heroin as "black woman." Sometimes they will substitute another word for woman, but still the color "black" refers to heroin and the color "white" refers to cocaine. Although not all messages are coded, it is important to be mindful of the possibility of a coded message when reviewing or monitoring mail written by inmates and gang and security threat group members.

Introduction

Contact Cards or Field Interview Cards (FI Cards), as they are better known, have been used by law enforcement officers for decades. Generally, Contact Cards are used to create a record of the contact itself and as a way to record the identifying characteristics of the individual who was contacted in case they need to be contacted later or to identify the individual contacted if their initial identification is questioned later. Contact Cards are also used to build statistics and analyze the type of people being contacted by law enforcement as well as where they are being contacted.

Gang and STG Contact Cards serve the same purpose as Contact Cards or Field Interview Cards. Gang and STG Contact Cards also serve the additional purpose of collecting not only identifying characteristics about an individual, but also the characteristics that identify that individual as a gang or STG member. Examples of the additional characteristics that are recorded on gang and STG Contact Cards include, but are not limited to, information about the person's gang/STG and set, their moniker, and their gang or STG related tattoos.

The bottom of every contact card has a list of categories related to gang or STG affiliation as well as a point value based on a ten (10) point system. An individual is awarded points for each of the categories there is proof of at the time of the contact. When the individual is awarded a total of ten (10) or more points the individual is considered a gang or STG member. Any individual that earns between one (1) and nine (9) points is considered an associate of a gang or STG. An individual scoring zero (0) points is assumed to have no affiliation with a gang or STG.

This information can be used to determine the size of a gang or STG, its racial makeup, the area the gang or STG is operating in, as well as a host of other information. Gang and STG Contact Cards are often the backbone of any Gang and or Intelligence Unit and cannot be replaced by other information-gathering techniques. Because of this fact the proper use of contact cards is essential to the success of any program designed to track and manage gangs and STGs.

The following are common examples of Contact Cards that are currently in use throughout the nation. Included are example Contact Cards that can be used in prison/jails and on the street.

Contact Card – Type One

Contact Card (A)

Booking #:__________ FBI #: _________ Date: _______
Last Name: __________ First Name: _________ DOB: ____
Address: ____________________ City: ______ State:____
SEX:___ Race:___ Hgt:__ Wgt:___ Eyes:____ Hair:____
Gang / STG:______________ Set:________ Moniker:________
Tattoos:____
Scars:___________________ Marks:_________________
Associates:______________ Contacting Officer:________
Ten Point Validation
Documents 5pts Publication 1pt Authorship 7pts Court Records 9pts Group Photo 2pts Association 2pts Contact 2pts Roll Call list 9pts Confidential Info 2pts Media 5pts Other Agencies 8pts Tattoos 7pts Self Admission 5pts Symbolism 2pts Total Points:____

Contact Card – Type Two

(Front) **Contact Card (B)**

Booking #:__________ FBI #: _________ Date: ______
Last Name: __________ First Name: _________ DOB: ____
Address: ____________________ City: ______ State:____
SEX:___ Race:___ Hgt:__ Wgt:___ Eyes:____ Hair:____
Gang / STG:_______________ Set:________ Moniker:________
Tattoos:____
Scars:___________________ Marks:_______________________
Associates:_______________ Contacting Officer:_________
Ten Point Validation
Documents 5pts Publication 1pt Authorship 7pts
Court Records 9pts Group Photo 2pts Association 2pts
Contact 2pts Roll Call list 9pts Confidential Info
2pts Media 5pts Other Agencies 8pts Tattoos 7pts
Self Admission 5pts Symbolism 2pts Total Points:____

(Back)

Right Thumb Print

Right Index Print

(Photo)

Contact Card – Type Three

Contact Card (B)

Booking #:______ Date: __________
FBI #: ________
Finger Print #: __________________

(Photo)

Last Name: _______________________
First Name: ______________________
DOB: ________
Address: _________________________
City: _______________ State:_____
SEX:___ Race:___ Hgt:__ Wgt:___ Eyes:____ Hair:____

Gang / STG:______________ Set:_______ Moniker:_______
Tattoos:____
Scars:__________________ Marks:________________________
Associates:______________ Contacting Officer:________

Ten Point Validation
Documents 5pts Publication 1pt Authorship 7pts Court Records 9pts Group Photo 2pts Association 2pts Contact 2pts Roll Call list 9pts Confidential Info 2pts Media 5pts Other Agencies 8pts Tattoos 7pts Self Admission 5pts Symbolism 2pts Total Points:____
Comments:____
____
____
____

Contact Card – Type Four *(Street 1)*

(Front) **Contact Card (Street 1)**

Date: ____________________ Time: ________________
Last Name: __________ First Name: _________ DOB: _____
Address: ____________________ City: ______ State:_____
SEX:___ Race:___ Hgt:__ Wgt:___ Eyes:____ Hair:____
Gang / STG:______________ Set:_______ Moniker:_______
Tattoos:____
Scars:__________________ Marks:_______________________
Contacting Officer:______________
Ten Point Validation
Documents 5pts Publication 1pt Authorship 7pts
Court Records 9pts Group Photo 2pts Association 2pts
Contact 2pts Roll Call list 9pts Confidential Info
2pts Media 5pts Other Agencies 8pts Tattoos 7pts
Self Admission 5pts Symbolism 2pts Total Points:____

(Back)

Vehicle Description:
Make:________________
Model: ________________
Year:________________
Color:________________

Comments:
____
____
____
____

Clothing Description:
Shirt:________________
Pants:________________
Shoes:________________
Mis:________________

Associates:
____
____
____
____

Contact Location:
Address:______________
____
____

Reason:______________
____
____

Contact Card – Type Five *(Street 2)*

(Front) **Contact Card (Street 2)**

Date: ____________________ Time: ________________
Last Name: __________ First Name: _________ DOB: _____
Address: ____________________ City: ______ State: _____
SEX:___ Race:___ Hgt:__ Wgt:___ Eyes:____ Hair:____
Gang / STG:_______________ Set:________ Moniker:________
Tattoos:____
Scars:____________________ Marks:_______________________
Contacting Officer:_______________

Vehicle Description:
Make:______________
Model: ______________
Year:______________
Color:______________

Clothing Description:
Shirt:______________
Pants:______________
Shoes:______________
Mis:______________

Associates:
____
____
____
____

(Back)

Ten Point Validation
Documents 5pts Publication 1pt Authorship 7pts
Court Records 9pts Group Photo 2pts Association 2pts
Contact 2pts Roll Call list 9pts Confidential Info
2pts Media 5pts Other Agencies 8pts Tattoos 7pts
Self Admission 5pts Symbolism 2pts Total Points:____

Comments:
____
____
____
____

Contact Location:
Address:______________
____
____

Reason:______________
____
____

Administrative Segregation (Ad-Seg): The removal of inmates from a prison's or jail's general population because of safety or security concerns, and placement in housing where inmates are locked in their cells for twenty-three hours a day with limited exposure to other inmates.

Aging out phenomena: The process by which a person grows out of criminal or gang behavior by taking part in more and more normal aspects of adulthood such as rasing a family and financial responsibilities.

Art: Graffiti.

Barrio: Neighborhood; the gang to which an Hispanic gang member belongs.

Bashing: A group assault on a single stranger carried out by racist skinheads based on the stranger's race or sexual orientation.

Black (woman): Refers to tar heroin.

B.L.O.O.D.: Brotherly Love Overriding Oppression and Destruction of Society (United Blood Nation)

Blood Line: Refers to any Latin King and Queen gangs outside of the Chicago, Illinois area.

Big Brother: The leader of a Asian street gang or high respected member.

Big Hommie: Refers to an O.G. member of a street gang or a gang sponsor; can also refer to a respected friend or mentor.

Big Six: Refers to the six largest outlaw motorcycle gangs in the world: The Hells Angels, the Bandidos, the Mongols, the Pagans, the Sons of Silence, and the Outlaws.

Cacique: The vice-president of a chapter of the Latin Kings.

Chapter: A branch or sub-set of a larger motorcycle club. Chapters can be found in both legitimate and illegitimate organizations.

Chicago Based Gangs: Refers to gangs that claim affiliation with either the Folk or People Nation.

Chicago Originals: Refers to the members of the Chicago based Almighty Latin King and Queen Nation.

Citizen: A word used to refer to people that are not involved with the criminal culture, as well as being ignorant about how it functions.

Clique: A subset or off shoot of a larger gang, security threat group, or umbrella gang.

Colors: A bandanna of a specific gang or security threat group color; a vest depicting the name, colors, and trademark or mascot of a Motorcycle Club or Gang.

Cook: A person who manufactures methamphetamine.

Crack: A solid form of cocaine resembling a white or yellowish colored rock.

Crank: A slang term for methamphetamines.

Crash Truck: A truck used by outlaw motorcycle gangs to follow the gang during required rides. The crash truck may contain motorcycle parts and contraband.

Crew: Another word for a gang or a group of individuals.

Corner Boys: Groups of individuals that loiter together on street corners.

Crab: A slang term used to show disrespect to Crip gang members.

Correctional Facility: A facility designed to house sentenced inmates; a jail or prison.

Crown Council: The governing and policy making body of the Latin Kings.

Cuts: A vest depicting the name, colors, and trademark, or mascot of a Motorcycle Club or Gang.

C.O.C.C.A. (Act): Colorado Organized Crime Control Act: the Colorado State racketeering law.

Dice In: A female gang or security threat group initiation where the female recruit is required to have sex with the same number of people as the number rolled on a set of dice.

Don: A mafia head or boss.

Donut(s): A slang term used to show disrespect to members of the Folk Nation; used to show disrespect to the GD. This term refers to the BGD leader, known as King David, being shot to death outside of a donut shop.

Down: Loyal, dedicated, ready to act.

Dressing Down: The wearing of gang or security threat group specific clothing; a gang or security threat group uniform.

Enforcer: A person who enforces the policies, discipline, rules, and regulations of a gang or security threat group.

Enforzador (Spanish): Enforce; a person who enforces the policies, discipline, rules, and regulations of a gang or security threat group.

Feeder Gang: Another term for puppet gang or puppet club; a gang that cultivates new members for a larger gang or security threat group.

Fifties (50's): Extremely large khakis or jeans, normally with a waist size of at least 50, worn by gang and security threat group members.

Flagging: A bandanna of a specific gang or security threat group color worn on or about the body of a gang or security threat group member.

Gang (traditional): Two or more individuals that may or may not be organized who commit delinquent or criminal activities that share a common name, theme, or look.

Gang (revised): Two or more individuals that may or may not be organized that commit delinquent or criminal activity and may or may not have a common name, theme or look, but are involved in furthering of the groups criminal activity.

Godfather: A member of criminal Tong or Triad that is mentor or adviser to a Asian street gang.

Hang Around: A person who is not a member or prospect member of an Outlaw Motorcycle Gang that spends their time associating with Outlaw Motorcycle Gangs and their members.

Hanging: The application of graffiti to a surface.

Heart: Refers to the bravery, internal fortitude, and loyalty of a person.

Headless Snake: A gang or security threat group that is capable of functioning without a structured or definitive leadership.

Hook(s): A slang term used to show disrespect to members of the People Nation. Refers to an upside down cane.

Huelas: Norteño small print or micro writing for the purpose of passing messages.

Inca: The president of a chapter of the Latin Kings.

Initiation: The process through which a member of a gang or security threat group is selected; generally through the testing of physical ability.

Investigador (Spanish): A person within a gang or security threat group that completes background checks of new members and carries out intelligence gathering operations.

Jail: A city or county maintained facility that houses presentence detainees and inmates serving sentences of a year or less.

Jumping In: A gang or security threat group initiation processes were a hopeful member is beaten by gang or security threat group members in order to prove their heart, bravery, and masculinity.

King: Refers to highest rank of the GDs and the LK's, i.e., King Hoover, King Tone, and King Shorty.

Launder: The act of taking illegal or illegitimate funds and changing them into legal or legitimate funds by investing them in a legitimate business and then retrieving the money from the business as profit or as a return on an investment or by some other legitimate means.

Loosely Organized: Members are a loosely affiliated group who share a minimum number of common goals and are only semi-loyal to the group and each other.

Mandatory Ride: A motorcycle trip all members of a motorcycle club are required to take part in under threat of punishment and/or monetary fine.

Motorcycle Club: A social club centered on the love of riding motorcycles and social interaction. Members of these clubs are not generally involved in criminal activity.

Nontraditional (Street) Gang: A gang whose members do not share a common cultural belief or a multigenerational connection.

Northern Structured Gangs: Refers to gangs that claims affiliation with the Norteño 14 or La Nuestra Familia.

Original Gangster or O.G.: Original Gangster refers to an original member of a street gang or an older member of a street gang.

Outlaw Motorcycle Gang or Club: A group of people involved in continuing criminal activity, with a group culture and personal lifestyle based round motorcycles and motorcycle history.

OMG: Abbreviation for Outlaw Motorcycle Gang or Club.

Organized: Members are a tightly affiliated group, share a larger number of common goals, and are loyal to the group. These groups are structured in much the same way as small businesses.

Party Crews: Small to medium size groups that sponsor and operate unofficial house parties.

Patching Over: Refers to the process of an Outlaw Motorcycle Club changing from an independent club to a puppet club or completely changing its name and becoming a local chapter of a larger club (i.e., the Brothers Fast "Patched Over" and became Denver first chapters of the Hells Angels).

Palaca (Spanish): A tag, moniker, nickname, or tattoo.

Pot Head: An avid user of marijuana.

Prison: A facility designed to house inmates serving sentences longer than a year in length.

Prospecting or Prospect Membership: An initiation process used by gangs and security threat groups where a current member sponsors, vouches for, or takes responsibility for a new member's character, loyalty, or actions.

Protection: A form of extortion paid by businesses to ensure the gang members do not disrupt their business (i.e., harassing customers, vandalism, or arson).

Puppet Club: An outlaw motorcycle gang sponsored by and acts as an agent of a larger outlaw motorcycle gang.

Puppet Gang: A gang that exclusively affiliates with and supports a larger gang or security threat group.

Putting in work: A gang or security threat group initiation where the hopeful gang or security threat group member is required to carry out serious criminal activity in order to prove themselves worthy of membership in the gang or security threat group.

P.O.W. Stands for Prisoners Of War.

Rave(s): Illegal underground parties based around the techno music culture and the use of designer drugs such as Ecstasy.

Representing: Showing one's affiliation with a gang or security threat group publicly through colors, signs, language, clothing, or any other means.

R.I.C.O. Act: Racketeer Influenced and Corrupt Organizations Act; a federal racketeering law.

Road Captain: The person in charge of planning and executing required rides for motorcycle clubs.

Run: A required trip taken by outlaw motorcycle gangs and motorcycle clubs.

Secretario (Spanish): Secretary.

Security Threat Group (traditional): An individual or a group of people that have a common disruptive goal; may share a common belief and are confined to a correctional facility.

Security Threat Group (revised): An individual or a group of people that have a common disruptive goal, may share a common belief, may or may not also be dedicated to furthering criminal activity, and are confined to a correctional facility.

Sergeant At Arms: A person within a motorcycle club that is responsible for enforcing club rules, policies, and regulations.

Sexing In: A gang or security threat group initiation that requires female recruits to either complete a sexual act or to have sex with or one or more members of the gang or group.

S.H.A.R.P.: Skin Heads Against Racial Prejudice

Semi-Organized: Members are a closely affiliated group, share a number of common goals and are only semi-loyal to the group.

Sign(s)(ing): Hand signs used to show gang affiliation.

Slob: A slang term used show disrespect to Blood gang members.

Soldier(s): The lowest member of a gang or security threat group; an entry level member of a gang or security threat group.

Southern Structured Gangs: Refers to gangs claiming affiliation with the Sureño 13 or the Mexican Mafia.

Speed: A slang term for methamphetamine.

STG: The abbreviation for Security Threat Group

Street Level Gang Member: A member of a gang and security threat group that has little knowledge of the group's overall organization and is involved only in the day-to-day criminal activity that allow the members to meet their own needs and still fulfill their small commitments to the gang or group.

Subculture: A group with values, social traits, and norms that are not generally accepted by the mainstream culture in a community.

Subset: An offshoot or a clique of a larger gang, security threat group, or umbrella gang.

Tagger: A person who is involved in the creation of graffiti.

Tagging Crew (Krew): Small groups of individuals, similar to a street gang, that are primarily involved in "hanging" graffiti.

Tesorero (Spanish): Treasure.

Tong (criminal): An Asian Organized Crime syndicate.

Traditional (Street) Gang: A multigenerational gang is made up of members of the same basic cultural or ethnic makeup.

Triad (criminal): An Asian Organized Crime syndicate.

Tribes: Refers to subsets of the Almighty Latin King and Queen Nation located outside of Chicago.

Turf: A specific area a gang or group determines to be their property or neighborhood.

Umbrella Gang: A large national gang that has several cliques or subsets (i.e., the Crips, the Sureño 13, and the Folk Nation).

Validate(ing)(tion): The legally excepted process of collecting information and intelligence on individuals that legally allows for the classification of an individual as a gang or security threat group member.

Weak: A slang term used to refer to a person who lacks loyalty or commitment to a gang, security threat group, friend, or co-defendant.

Well-Organized: Members are a tightly affiliated group, share common goals based on the success of organization, and are fiercely loyal to the group and each other. These groups are structured along the lines of an international business.

White (woman): Refers to cocaine.

Work (putting in work): Refers to the act of committing illegal activity on behalf of the gang or STG.

OTHER TITLES OF INTEREST FROM LOOSELEAF LAW PUBLICATIONS, INC.

Lou Savelli Pocket Guide Series

Gangs Across America and Their Symbols
Street Drugs
Graffiti

International Sex Trafficking of Women & Children
Understanding the Global Epidemic
by Leonard Territo and George Kirkham

Processing Under Pressure
Stress, Memory and Decision-Making in Law Enforcement
by Matthew J. Sharps

The Racial Profiling Controversy
What Every Police Leader Should Know
by Brian L. Withrow

Juvenile Justice Guide
by Edward A. Thibault, Ph.D. and John J. Maceri, MSW

Handgun Combatives
by Dave Spaulding

Police Tactical Life Saver
Crucial Skills for Handling Major Medical Crises
by Glenn French

Use of Force
Expert Guidance for Decisive Force Response
by Brian A. Kinnaird

Conflict Resolution for Law Enforcement
Street-Smart Negotiating
by Kyle E. Blanchfield, Thomas A. Blanchfield, and Peter D. Ladd

Citizens Terrorism Awareness and Survival
by Col. Michael Licata, USAF (Ret.)